Practice and Homework Journal

Grade 3

1 Understand Multiplication and Area

Module 1 Understand Multiplication

Lesson 1 Count Equal Groups.. P1

Lesson 2 Relate Addition and Multiplication P3

Lesson 3 Represent Multiplication with Arrays P5

Lesson 4 Understand the Commutative Property of Multiplication P7

Lesson 5 Represent Multiplication with Number Lines P9

Lesson 6 Represent Multiplication with Bar Models P11

Module 2 Relate Multiplication and Area

Lesson 1 Understand Area by Counting Unit Squares P13

Lesson 2 Measure Area by Counting Unit Squares............................ P15

Lesson 3 Relate Area to Addition and Multiplication......................... P17

Lesson 4 Solve Problems with Area.. P19

Lesson 5 Find the Area of Combined Rectangles P21

Multiplication and Division

Module 3 Understand Multiplication Strategies

Lesson 1 Multiply with 2 and 4 .... **P23**

Lesson 2 Multiply with 5 and 10... **P25**

Lesson 3 Multiply with 3 and 6 .... **P27**

Module 4 Apply Multiplication Properties as Strategies

Lesson 1 Understand the Identity and Zero Properties of Multiplication **P29**

Lesson 2 Understand the Distributive Property................................. **P31**

Lesson 3 Understand the Associative Property of Multiplication **P33**

Lesson 4 Multiply with 7 .... **P35**

Lesson 5 Multiply with 8 .... **P37**

Lesson 6 Multiply with 9 .... **P39**

Lesson 7 Identify Number Patterns on the Multiplication Table **P41**

Module 5 Multiplication with Multiples of 10

Lesson 1 Use the Distributive Property **P43**

Lesson 2 Use the Associative Property of Multiplication....................... **P45**

Lesson 3 Use Place-Value Strategies to Multiply with Multiples of 10 .... **P47**

Lesson 4 Multiply Multiples of 10 by 1-Digit Numbers......................... **P49**

© Houghton Mifflin Harcourt Publishing Company

Module 6 Understand Division

Lesson 1 Represent Division **P51**

Lesson 2 Separate Objects into Equal Groups **P53**

Lesson 3 Find the Number of Equal Groups **P55**

Lesson 4 Relate Subtraction and Division **P57**

Lesson 5 Represent Division with Arrays **P59**

Lesson 6 Represent Division with Bar Models **P61**

Lesson 7 Apply Division Rules for 1 and 0 . . . . **P63**

Module 7 Relate Multiplication and Division

Lesson 1 Relate Multiplication and Division **P65**

Lesson 2 Write Related Facts **P67**

Lesson 3 Multiply and Divide with 2, 4, and 8 . . . . **P69**

Lesson 4 Multiply and Divide with 5 and 10 . . . . **P71**

Lesson 5 Multiply and Divide with 3 and 6 . . . . **P73**

Lesson 6 Multiply and Divide with 7 and 9 . . . . **P75**

Lesson 7 Build Fluency with Multiplication and Division **P77**

Module 8 Apply Multiplication and Division

Lesson 1 Identify and Extend Patterns **P79**

Lesson 2 Find Unknown Factors and Numbers **P81**

Lesson 3 Use Multiplication and Division to Solve Problem Situations **P83**

Lesson 4 Solve Two-Step Problems **P85**

Lesson 5 Practice with One- and Two-Step Problems **P87**

Unit 3 Addition and Subtraction Strategies and Applications

Module 9 Addition and Subtraction Strategies

Lesson 1 Identify Number Patterns on the Addition Table......................**P89**

Lesson 2 Use Mental Math Strategies for Addition and Subtraction...........**P91**

Lesson 3 Use Properties to Add...**P93**

Lesson 4 Use Mental Math to Assess Reasonableness..........................**P95**

Lesson 5 Round to the Nearest Ten or Hundred...............................**P97**

Lesson 6 Use Estimation with Sums and Differences..........................**P99**

Module 10 Addition and Subtraction Within 1,000

Lesson 1 Use Expanded Form to Add..**P101**

Lesson 2 Use Place Value to Add...**P103**

Lesson 3 Combine Place Values to Subtract..................................**P105**

Lesson 4 Use Place Value to Subtract.......................................**P107**

Lesson 5 Choose a Strategy to Add or Subtract..............................**P109**

Lesson 6 Model and Solve Two-Step Problems................................**P111**

Module 11 Understand Perimeter

Lesson 1 Describe Perimeter...**P113**

Lesson 2 Find Perimeter...**P115**

Lesson 3 Find Unknown Side Lengths...**P117**

Lesson 4 Represent Rectangles with the Same Area
and Different Perimeters..**P119**

Lesson 5 Represent Rectangles with the Same Perimeter
and Different Areas...**P121**

Module 12 Time Measurement and Intervals

Lesson 1 Tell and Write Time to the Minute **P123**

Lesson 2 Use a.m. and p.m. to Describe Time **P125**

Lesson 3 Measure Time Intervals **P127**

Lesson 4 Find Start and End Times... **P129**

Lesson 5 Solve Time Interval Problems...................................... **P131**

Unit 4 Fractions

Module 13 Understand Fractions as Numbers

Lesson 1 Describe Equal Parts of a Whole **P133**

Lesson 2 Represent and Name Unit Fractions.............................. **P135**

Lesson 3 Represent and Name Fractions of a Whole....................... **P137**

Lesson 4 Represent and Name Fractions on a Number Line................. **P139**

Lesson 5 Express Whole Numbers as Fractions............................. **P141**

Lesson 6 Represent and Name Fractions Greater Than 1 .... **P143**

Lesson 7 Use Fractions to Measure Lengths................................ **P145**

Module 14 Relate Shapes, Fractions, and Area

Lesson 1 Relate Fractions and Area...................................... **P147**

Lesson 2 Partition Shapes into Equal Areas................................ **P149**

Lesson 3 Use Unit Fractions to Describe Area.............................. **P151**

Module 15 Compare Fractions

Lesson 1 Compare Fractions Using Concrete and Visual Models **P153**

Lesson 2 Compare Fractions with the Same Denominator................... **P155**

Lesson 3 Compare Fractions with the Same Numerator **P157**

Lesson 4 Use Reasoning Strategies to Compare Fractions **P159**

Module 16 Understand Equivalent Fractions

Lesson 1 Represent Equivalent Fractions with Smaller Parts **P161**

Lesson 2 Represent Equivalent Fractions with Larger Parts **P163**

Lesson 3 Recognize and Generate Equivalent Fractions **P165**

Unit 5 Measurement and Data

Module 17 Liquid Volume and Mass

Lesson 1 Estimate and Measure Liquid Volume............................. P167

Lesson 2 Estimate and Measure Mass.................................... P169

Lesson 3 Solve Problems About Liquid Volume and Mass.................... P171

Module 18 Represent and Interpret Data

Lesson 1 Use Picture Graphs.. P173

Lesson 2 Make Picture Graphs.. P175

Lesson 3 Use Bar Graphs... P177

Lesson 4 Make Bar Graphs P179

Lesson 5 Use Line Plots to Display Measurement Data...................... P181

Lesson 6 Make Line Plots to Display Measurement Data P183

Lesson 7 Solve One- and Two-Step Problems Using Data P185

Unit 6 Geometry

Module 19 Define Two-Dimensional Shapes

Lesson 1 Describe Shapes.. P187

Lesson 2 Describe Angles in Shapes P189

Lesson 3 Describe Sides of Shapes P191

Lesson 4 Define Quadrilaterals P193

Module 20 Categorize Two-Dimensional Shapes

Lesson 1 Draw Quadrilaterals P195

Lesson 2 Categorize Quadrilaterals.. P197

Lesson 3 Categorize Plane Shapes P199

My Math Journal.. J1

My Progress on Mathematics Standards J2

My Learning Summary.. J12

Interactive Glossary.. J33

Table of Measures.. J63

© Houghton Mifflin Harcourt Publishing Company

Name _____

LESSON 1.1
**More Practice/
Homework**

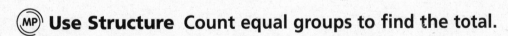
ONLINE
Video Tutorials and
Interactive Examples

Count Equal Groups

1 (MP) **Use Tools** Abe is growing 5 plants.
Each plant has 6 leaves. How many
leaves are there?

- Draw a visual model.

- Describe your visual model.

  _____

  _____

  _____

  _____

- How many leaves are there?

  _____

2 (MP) **Attend to Precision** Toshi has 9 planters with
4 plants in each planter.

- Write the numbers you say when you count by
  4s to find how many plants there are.

  _____

- How many plants are there?

  _____

(MP) **Use Structure** Count equal groups to find the total.

3

4

_____ groups of _____ blocks   _____ groups of _____ blocks

_____ blocks   _____ blocks

Test Prep

5 Shanti makes 4 equal groups of apples. Each group has 3 apples. Which visual model represents the problem?

Ⓐ

Ⓑ

Ⓒ

Ⓓ

6 Luis buys 7 shirts. What is the cost of the 7 shirts?

Ⓐ $56   Ⓒ $28

Ⓑ $49   Ⓓ $15

Sporty Clothing Store	
Item	Price
Shorts	$7
Socks	$4
Shirt	$8

7 Tonya has 6 toy cars. Each toy car has 4 wheels. Describe a visual model Tonya can draw to show equal groups.

_____

_____

_____

Spiral Review

Choose a strategy to add or subtract.

8 37 + 23 = _____   **9** 62 − 48 = _____   **10**   24
                                                                              49
                                                                          + 5

Relate Addition and Multiplication

1 (MP) **Model with Mathematics** There are 5 teams competing in a race. Each team has 4 runners. How many runners are in the race? Write an addition equation to model the problem.

_____

2 Each sheet has 8 stamps. There are 3 sheets. How many stamps are on the 3 sheets? Show equal groups. Write an addition equation and a multiplication equation.

Add. _____ + _____ + _____ = _____ stamps

Multiply. _____ × _____ = _____ stamps

3 **Math on the Spot** Thomas bought 3 apples. Sydney bought 5 peaches. Which weighed more—the 3 apples or the 5 peaches? How much more? Explain how you know.

Average Weight of Fruits	
Fruit	**Weight in Ounces**
Apple	6
Orange	5
Peach	3
Banana	4

_____

_____

_____

4 (MP) **Attend to Precision** Trent writes $10 \times 6 = 60$ to find the number of muffins in 10 boxes. Describe what each of the factors represents in the multiplication equation.

_____

_____

_____

Test Prep

5 Trina fills 6 prize bags. Each prize bag has 5 rings. How many rings are in the 6 bags? Select all the equations that model the problem.

Ⓐ $6 \times 5 = 30$

Ⓑ $5 \times 6 = 30$

Ⓒ $6 + 6 + 6 + 6 + 6 = 30$

Ⓓ $5 + 5 + 5 + 5 + 5 + 5 = 30$

Ⓔ $6 + 5 = 11$

6 Mr. Leo puts 8 bags of potting soil in his truck. What is the weight of 8 bags of potting soil?

Ⓐ 15 pounds

Ⓑ 56 pounds

Ⓒ 64 pounds

Ⓓ 72 pounds

Sunshine Garden Shop	
Bags	**Weight in Pounds**
Potting Soil	7
Clover Seeds	5
Grass Seeds	9

7 Jamar writes $4 \times 6 = 24$ to find the total number of marbles he has. How might Jamar describe what each factor represents in the multiplication equation?

_____

_____

_____

Spiral Review

8 Jose takes 17 shells out of a box. There are 38 shells in the box now. How many shells were in the box to start?

_____

9 What number makes the equation true?

$23 + 5 = $ _____ $ + 18$

Represent Multiplication with Arrays

1 (MP) **Model with Mathematics** Mr. Bloom grows vegetables in his garden.

Mr. Bloom's Garden	
Vegetable	**Planted In**
Beans	4 rows of 6
Carrots	2 rows of 8
Corn	5 rows of 9
Beets	4 rows of 7

- Write a multiplication equation for growing corn. How many corn plants does Mr. Bloom have in his garden?

  _____

- **Math on the Spot** Could Mr. Bloom have planted his beans in equal rows of 3? If so, how many rows could he have planted? Explain.

  _____

  _____

  _____

  _____

2 (MP) **Use Tools** A chessboard has 8 squares in each row. There are 8 rows. How many squares are on the chessboard? Draw an array for the problem. Write a multiplication equation.

  _____

3 **Open Ended** Write and solve a word problem about a 2 × 5 array.

  _____

  _____

  _____

Test Prep

4 The band members stand in an 8 × 6 rectangular arrangement. Which sentence can be used to describe the arrangement?

Ⓐ There are 48 rows of 6 band members.

Ⓑ There are 6 rows of 8 band members.

Ⓒ There are a total of 14 band members.

Ⓓ There are a total of 48 band members.

5 Elsa draws an array to show squares on a game board. Select all the factors in the multiplication equation that model Elsa's array.

Ⓐ 2

Ⓑ 3

Ⓒ 4

Ⓓ 5

Ⓔ 10

6 Each row on a sheet of stickers has 3 stickers. There are 7 rows. How many stickers are on the sheet? Describe an array that shows this problem.

_____

Spiral Review

Find the sum or difference.

7 5 + 7 = _____

8 15 − 9 = _____

9 Write *even* or *odd* to describe the number of tiles.

_____

Name _____

LESSON 1.4
**More Practice/
Homework**

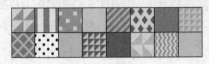
ONLINE
Video Tutorials and
Interactive Examples

Understand the Commutative Property of Multiplication

1 (MP) **Model with Mathematics** Kali arranges quilt squares in 2 rows with 8 squares in each row. Dan arranges quilt squares in 8 rows with 2 squares in each row. How many quilt squares does Dan use?

- Draw an array to show the problem.

- Write an equation for your array. How many quilt squares does Dan use?

_____

Draw an array. Then write related equations to show the Commutative Property of Multiplication.

2 (MP) **Use Tools** Akani places tiles on a wall. She places 7 tiles in each row. There are 4 rows. How many tiles are on the wall?

Multiplication Equation   Related Multiplication Equation

_____   _____

(MP) **Use Structure** Write the unknown factor.

3 $9 \times 7 = \boxed{} \times 9$ **4** $10 \times 8 = 8 \times \boxed{}$

5 **Open Ended** Write a multiplication equation. Explain how you can use the Commutative Property of Multiplication to write the related multiplication equation. Write both multiplication equations.

_____

_____

_____

Test Prep

6 Kim's game board has 7 rows with 4 squares in each row. Juan's game board has 4 rows with 7 squares in each row. Select all the equations that model Kim's or Juan's game board.

Ⓐ $4 \times 4 = 16$

Ⓑ $7 \times 7 = 49$

Ⓒ $8 \times 4 = 32$

Ⓓ $4 \times 7 = 28$

Ⓔ $7 \times 4 = 28$

7 What is the unknown number in the equation?

$5 \times 9 = 9 \times \blacksquare$

Ⓐ 5   Ⓒ 14

Ⓑ 9   Ⓓ 45

8 Draw lines to match the array to the correct equation.

   •   • $3 \times 2 = 6$

   •   • $2 \times 3 = 6$

Spiral Review

9 Write the time.

10 Draw lines to separate the shape into 4 equal parts.

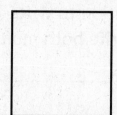

Name _____

Represent Multiplication with Number Lines

1 (MP) **Use Tools** Jerome uses 4 paper clips to measure the length of a watch. Each paper clip is 5 centimeters long. How many centimeters long is the watch?

• Show equal groups on the number line.

0 1 2 3 4 5 6 7 8 9 10 11 12 13 14 15 16 17 18 19 20

• How many centimeters long is the watch?

_____

2 (MP) **Model with Mathematics** Each string is 9 inches long. Tia uses 2 strings to measure the length of a necklace. What is the length of the necklace in inches?

• Show equal groups on the number line. Write a multiplication equation. Solve.

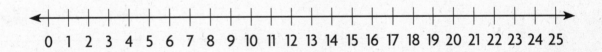

0 1 2 3 4 5 6 7 8 9 10 11 12 13 14 15 16 17 18 19 20 21 22 23 24 25

_____

3 (MP) **Reason** Rob uses 10 rulers to measure the length of a bicycle. Each ruler is 6 inches long. How can you use a number line and multiplication to find the length of the bicycle in inches?

_____

_____

Test Prep

4 Asha uses 4 strings to measure the length of a desk. Each string is 8 centimeters long. How many centimeters long is the desk? Select all the equations that model the problem.

Ⓐ $4 \times 8 = \blacksquare$ Ⓓ $8 + 8 + 8 + 8 = \blacksquare$

Ⓑ $8 \times 4 = \blacksquare$ Ⓔ $4 + 4 + 4 + 4 + 4 + 4 + 4 + 4 = \blacksquare$

Ⓒ $8 \times 8 = \blacksquare$

5 A measuring stick is 3 feet long. Coby uses 9 measuring sticks to measure the length of a truck. What is the length of the truck in feet?

Ⓐ 12 feet

Ⓑ 24 feet

Ⓒ 27 feet

Ⓓ 30 feet

6 Romi measures the length of a ribbon using 7 index cards. Each index card is 5 inches long. How many inches long is the ribbon? Write and solve an equation to model the problem.

_____

Spiral Review

7 Miguel uses 3 dimes, 5 nickels, and 2 pennies to buy a marble. What is the total value of the coins?

_____ ¢

8 How many sides and vertices does a triangle have?

_____ sides

_____ vertices

Name _____

LESSON 1.6
**More Practice/
Homework**

ONLINE
Video Tutorials and
Interactive Examples

Represent Multiplication
with Bar Models

1 (MP) **Model with Mathematics** Kareem makes
5 bracelets for a craft show. Each bracelet has 4 beads.
How many beads does Kareem use?

• Draw a bar model to show the problem.

• How do you know what number to write inside
each box?

_____

_____

• Write a multiplication equation and solve the problem.
How many beads does Kareem use?

_____

2 (MP) **Use Tools** Each classroom has 3 windows. There are
6 classrooms. How many windows are in 6 classrooms?

Draw a bar model. Write a multiplication equation.

_____

How many windows are in 6 classrooms? _____

3 **Math on the Spot** Suppose there are 3 groups of
4 trumpet players. In front of the trumpet players are
9 saxophone players. How many students play the
trumpet or saxophone?

_____

Test Prep

4 Each van has 8 seats. There are 4 vans. How many seats are there? Kendra drew this bar model for the problem. Select all the statements that match the information.

Ⓐ There are 4 objects in each group.

Ⓑ There are 8 objects in each group.

Ⓒ There are 4 groups.

Ⓓ There are 8 groups.

Ⓔ There are 32 objects.

| 8 | 8 | 8 | 8 |

■ seats

5 There are 7 swim teams. Each team has 5 swimmers. How many swimmers are on the 7 teams?

Ⓐ 2

Ⓑ 12

Ⓒ 35

Ⓓ 40

6 Tim packs 6 lunch bags. He puts 2 pieces of fruit in each bag. How many pieces of fruit does Tim pack?

_____

Spiral Review

7 There are 9 cars. Each car has 4 wheels. How many wheels are there?

_____ groups of _____ wheels

_____ wheels

8 There are 3 horses in a field. Each horse has 4 legs. Write an addition equation and a multiplication equation to find the number of legs on 3 horses.

Add: _____

Multiply: _____

Understand Area by Counting Unit Squares

1 **Open-Ended** Draw two different figures, each with an area of 10 square units.

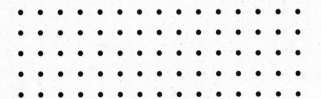

Count to find the area of the figure.

2

3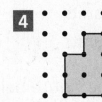

4

_____ square units   _____ square units   _____ square units

5 Keiko draws this figure.

- What is the area of the figure? _____ square units

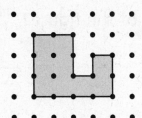

- **MP** **Reason** Show a different figure that has the same area as Keiko's figure.

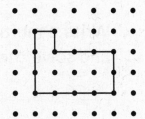

Test Prep

6 Tricia drew the figure below. Which is the area of the figure?

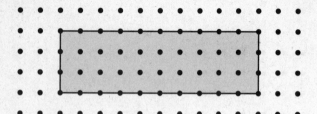

- Ⓐ 10 square units
- Ⓑ 27 square units
- Ⓒ 30 square units
- Ⓓ 36 square units

7 Victor drew the figure below.

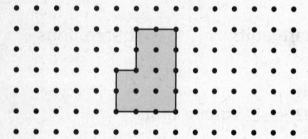

What is the area, in square units, of the figure?

_____

Spiral Review

8 There are 5 sailboats in a race. Each boat has 4 team members. How many team members are in the race?

Add. _____

Multiply. _____

_____

9 The band is seated in 3 rows. Each row has 4 chairs. How many chairs are there?

Write a multiplication equation and solve the problem.

_____

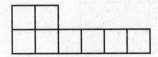
Measure Area by Counting Unit Squares

1 (MP) **Construct Arguments** Each unit square in the figure is 1 square inch. Lance says that the figure has an area of 6 square inches. Is Lance correct? Explain.

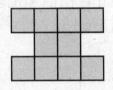

_____

_____

Count to find the area of the figure.

2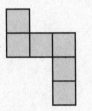

Area = _____
square inches

3

Area = _____
square centimeters

4

Area = _____
square inches

5 **Math on the Spot** You measure the area of a tabletop with blue unit squares and green unit squares. Which unit square will give you a greater number of square units for area? Explain.

blue   green

_____

_____

Test Prep

6 Wes made a design using tiles. Each tile is 1 square inch. Which is the area of the design?

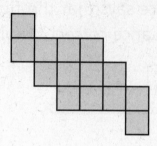

- (A) 11 square inches
- (B) 12 square inches
- (C) 13 square inches
- (D) 14 square inches

7 Ashley drew the figure shown using unit squares. Each unit square is 1 square centimeter.

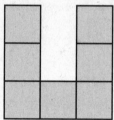

What is the area of the figure?

Spiral Review

8 Each group of students has 2 markers. There are 5 groups. How many markers are there?

Write a multiplication equation, and then solve the problem.

9 Write the unknown factor.

$6 \times 4 = \boxed{} \times 6$

Relate Area to Addition and Multiplication

1 (MP) **Use Repeated Reasoning** Connor is measuring a rectangular picture using unit squares. Each unit square is 1 square inch. So far, he has made 3 rows with 5 unit squares in each row. He sees that there will be 2 more rows of 5. Explain how Connor can use multiplication to find the area of the picture.

_____

_____

Find the area of the figure. Show repeated addition. Show multiplication.

2 Each unit square is 1 square foot.

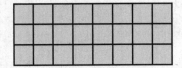

3 Each unit square is 1 square inch.

Add. _____

Multiply. _____

Area = _____

Add. _____

Multiply. _____

Area = _____

4 **Math on the Spot** A tile company tiles a wall using square tiles. A mural is painted in the center. The drawing shows the design. The area of each tile used is 1 square foot.

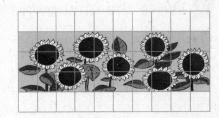

Write a problem that can be solved by using the drawing. Then solve your problem.

_____

_____

Test Prep

5 A card is in the shape of the rectangle shown.

Each unit square is 1 square inch.

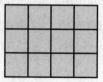

Which is the area of the card?

Ⓐ 12 square inches

Ⓑ 7 square inches

Ⓒ 4 square inches

Ⓓ 3 square inches

6 Binh uses unit squares to measure the area of a playground. Each unit square is 1 square foot. What is the area of the playground?

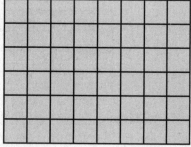

_____

Spiral Review

7 Write the unknown factor.

$9 \times 3 = \boxed{} \times 9$

8 Mia measures a bicycle, which is equal to the length of 3 sticks. Each stick is 2 feet long. How long is Mia's bicycle?

_____

LESSON 2.4
**More Practice/
Homework**

😊Ed **ONLINE**
Video Tutorials and
Interactive Examples

Solve Problems with Area

1 (MP) **Reason** A poster in the shape of a rectangle has an area of 12 square feet. One of the side lengths is 4 feet. Write an equation to find the unknown side length. Then solve.

_____

Find the area of the rectangle. Write a multiplication equation.

2

5 inches

5 inches

3 3 centimeters

5 centimeters

Multiply. _____

Area = _____

Multiply. _____

Area = _____

4 **Art** Carl measures two rectangular murals. One mural is shown. Multiply to find the area of this mural.

_____

The other mural has one side length of 2 feet and another side length of 4 feet. Multiply to find the area of the other mural.

Compare the areas. Which mural has a greater area?

_____

_____

6 ft.

1 ft.

Test Prep

5 A garden is in the shape of the rectangle shown.

3 meters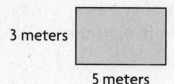

5 meters

What is the area of the garden?

_____

6 A rectangle has a side length of 4 feet and another side length of 5 feet. What is the area of the rectangle?

(A) 4 square feet

(B) 9 square feet

(C) 20 square feet

(D) 25 square feet

Spiral Review

7 Miya measures a rug that is equal to the length of 2 pieces of string. The length of each piece of string is 4 feet. What is the total length of the rug?

_____

8 Each basket has 6 crayons. There are 4 baskets. How many crayons are there?

_____

Name _____

Find the Area of Combined Rectangles

1 (MP) **Attend to Precision** Felicia draws this diagram of a kitchen floor. What is the area of the kitchen?

_____

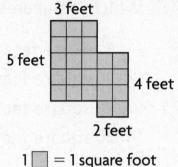

3 feet

5 feet

4 feet

2 feet

1 ▢ = 1 square foot

Draw a line to break apart the figure into rectangles. Find the area of the figure.

2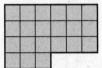

1 ▢ = 1 square meter

Area = _____ square meters

3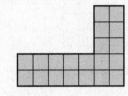

1 ▢ = 1 square inch

Area = _____ square inches

4 **Math on the Spot** Explain how to break apart the figure to find the area.

_____

_____

_____

_____

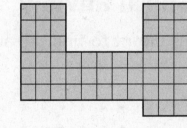

Test Prep

5 The floor of a room is shown.

Which is the area of the floor?

Ⓐ 6 square feet

Ⓑ 20 square feet

Ⓒ 26 square feet

Ⓓ 30 square feet

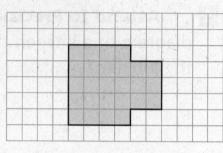

1 ☐ = 1 square foot

Find the area of each figure.

6

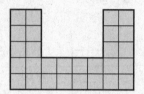

1 ☐ = 1 square centimeter

7

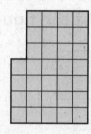

1 ☐ = 1 square inch

_____

_____

Spiral Review

8 Count to find the area of the figure.

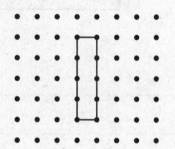

_____ square units

9 What is the related multiplication equation?

$9 \times 7 = 63$

_____

LESSON 3.1
**More Practice/
Homework**

ONLINE
Video Tutorials and
Interactive Examples

Multiply with 2 and 4

1 There are 5 reading groups in Mrs. Smith's class.
Each group reads 2 books. How many books do
the 5 groups read? Draw the jumps on the number line.

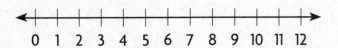

0 1 2 3 4 5 6 7 8 9 10 11 12

- The groups read _____ books.

Use a 2s fact and doubling to find the product.

2 4 × 4 = ◼

2 × 4 = _____

_____ + _____ = _____

4 × 4 = _____

3 4 × 10 = ◼

2 × 10 = _____

_____ + _____ = _____

4 × 10 = _____

4 (MP) **Attend to Precision** There are 4 tables. Each table
has 8 chairs. How many chairs are there? Show and
describe the steps you used to solve the problem.

_____

_____

5 (MP) **Attend to Precision** Lindsey, Louis, Sally, and Matt
each bring 5 guests to the school play. How many
guests do they bring to the school play? Explain.

_____

_____

Test Prep

6 Ava buys some yarn and cuts it into 8 pieces that are the same length. Each piece is 2 feet long. How many feet of yarn does Ava buy?

Ⓐ 16 feet   Ⓒ 6 feet

Ⓑ 10 feet   Ⓓ 4 feet

7 Edgar is having a dinner party. Each table has 4 chairs. Edgar's friends fill 5 tables. How many of Edgar's friends are at his dinner party?

Ⓐ 9   Ⓒ 20

Ⓑ 10   Ⓓ 25

8 Marco has 2 picture frames on each wall. Each frame has 10 pictures. How many pictures are on 2 walls? Select all the statements that match the problem.

Ⓐ There are 2 × 10 pictures on each wall.

Ⓑ There are 2 × 10 pictures on two walls.

Ⓒ There are 4 × 10 pictures on each wall.

Ⓓ There are 4 × 10 pictures on two walls.

Ⓔ There are 2 × 2 pictures on each wall.

Spiral Review

9 Count to find the area of the figure. Each unit square is 1 square meter.

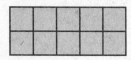

Area = _____ square meters

10 Find the area of the figure. Each unit square is 1 square yard.

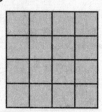

Area = _____

LESSON 3.2
**More Practice/
Homework**

ONLINE
Video Tutorials and
Interactive Examples

Multiply with 5 and 10

1 (MP) **Use Tools** Liz makes 3 programs for a play that the drama club is performing. Each program has 10 pages. How many pages are in the 3 programs?

- Show how you can solve the problem.

- There are _____ pages in the 3 programs.

2 (MP) **Reason** How can you use a number line to find the first 5 multiples of 5? _____

0   5   10   15   20   25   30   35   40   45   50

- 5, _____, _____, _____, _____

- What is the product 5×5? _____

3 (MP) **Attend to Precision** The orchestra has 5 violins and 3 banjos that need new strings. How many strings need to be replaced? Explain.

Stringed Instruments	
Instrument	Strings
Guitar	6
Banjo	5
Mandolin	8
Violin	4

_____

_____

4 **STEM** The metric system is based on multiples of 10. Which unit of length in the metric system is equal to 10×10 centimeters?

Metric Units of Length	
Unit	Number of Centimeters
Decimeter	10
Meter	100

_____

Test Prep

5 Fred says that he skates 5 miles in one hour. This week he skates for 7 hours. How many miles does Fred skate?

Ⓐ 2 miles   Ⓒ 35 miles

Ⓑ 12 miles   Ⓓ 40 miles

6 Kayla collects blankets for an animal shelter. She fills 9 boxes. There are 10 blankets in each box. How many blankets does Kayla collect for the shelter? Select all that represent the total number of blankets.

Ⓐ 9 × 10 blankets

Ⓑ 9 + 10 blankets

Ⓒ 10 + 9 blankets

Ⓓ 9 + 9 + 9 + 9 + 9 + 9 + 9 + 9 + 9 + 9 blankets

Ⓔ 10 + 10 + 10 + 10 + 10 + 10 + 10 + 10 + 10 blankets

7 Wai has 6 nickels. The value of a nickel is 5 cents. What is the value of Wai's nickels in cents? Write a multiplication equation and solve the problem.

Spiral Review

8 An equation is shown.

6 × 4 = 4 × ■

What is the unknown number?

■ = _____

9 Find the area of the figure.

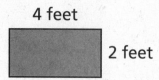

4 feet

2 feet

Area = _____

Multiply with 3 and 6

1 (MP) **Use Tools** Sara scores 3 goals in each soccer game. She plays 8 soccer games. How many goals does she score? Show the equal groups.

8 × _____ = _____

Sara scores _____ goals.

2 (MP) **Use Structure** There are 6 houses on the street. Each house has 5 windows. How many windows are on the 6 houses?

Find the product using a 3s fact and doubling.

6 × 5 = ■

_____

There are _____ windows.

Use the multiplication table to find the product.

3 3 × 4 = _____   **4** 3 × 8 = _____

5 6 × 4 = _____   **6** 6 × 8 = _____

×	1	2	3	4	5	6	7	8	9	10
1	1	2	3	4	5	6	7	8	9	10
2	2	4	6	8	10	12	14	16	18	20
3	3	6	9		15	18	21		27	30
4	4	8		16	20		28	32	36	40
5	5	10	15	20	25	30	35	40	45	50
6	6	12	18		30	36	42		54	60
7	7	14	21	28	35	42	49	56	63	70
8	8	16		32	40		56	64	72	80
9	9	18	27	36	45	54	63	72	81	90
10	10	20	30	40	50	60	70	80	90	100

7 **Math on the Spot** Alli uses some craft sticks to make shapes. If she uses one craft stick for each side of the shape, would Alli use more craft sticks for 6 squares or 8 triangles? Explain.

_____

Test Prep

8 Antonio uses tape to fix an art project. He cuts the tape into 6 pieces that are the same length. Each piece of tape is 9 inches long. How many inches of tape does Antonio use to fix the project?

(A) 15 inches (B) 45 inches (C) 54 inches (D) 60 inches

9 The cost of a movie ticket is $6. What is the cost for 7 movie tickets?

(A) $13 (B) $28 (C) $36 (D) $42

10 Some friends are making snack kits for a hiking trip. They place 6 bottles of water and 5 granola bars in each kit. There are 3 kits. Select all the sentences that describe the snack kits.

(A) There are 3 groups of 3 granola bars in the snack kits.

(B) There are 3 groups of 5 granola bars in the snack kits.

(C) There are 6 groups of 3 granola bars in the snack kits.

(D) There are 3 groups of 6 water bottles in the snack kits.

(E) There are 6 groups of 5 water bottles in the snack kits.

Spiral Review

Draw a line to break apart the figure into rectangles. Find the area of the figure. Show multiplication and addition equations.

11

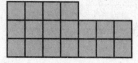

Area = _____ square units

12

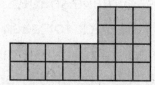

Area = _____ square units

Understand the Identity and Zero Properties of Multiplication

1 (MP) **Model with Mathematics** Rex has 6 cartons. Each carton has 0 eggs. How many eggs are in the cartons?

- Draw to show equal groups.

- Write a multiplication equation.

_____

- How many eggs are in the cartons?

_____

Complete the equation. Solve.

2 Ji makes a vase of flowers. She puts 10 flowers in the vase. How many flowers are there?

_____ × _____ = _____

There are _____ flowers in the vase.

3 Each carton has 0 bottles of juice. There are 5 cartons. How many bottles of juice are in the cartons?

_____ × _____ = _____

There are _____ bottles of juice.

Find the product.

4 $0 \times 7 = \boxed{}$ **5** $1 \times 9 = \boxed{}$ **6** $\boxed{} = 6 \times 1$

7 **Open Ended** Write a word problem that can be solved using the equation $0 \times 4 = 0$. Then solve.

_____

_____

Test Prep

8 A package has 3 beads. Sela buys 1 package. Bret buys 0 packages. Select the equations that describe the number of beads they each buy.

Ⓐ $0 \times 1 = 0$ Ⓓ $1 \times 3 = 3$

Ⓑ $0 \times 3 = 0$ Ⓔ $3 \times 1 = 3$

Ⓒ $3 \times 0 = 0$

9 An equation is shown.

$1 \times 5 = \blacksquare$

What is the unknown number?

Ⓐ 0   Ⓑ 1   Ⓒ 5   Ⓓ 6

10 Draw lines to match the fact on the left to the correct product.

4×1 •   • 0

8×0 •   • 2

1×2 •   • 4

Spiral Review

11 There are 4 boxes of markers. Each box has 9 markers. How many markers are there?

Write an addition equation and a multiplication equation.

Add: _____

Multiply: _____

There are _____ markers.

12 Each bag of flour weighs 5 pounds. What is the weight of 3 bags of flour?

Write an addition equation and a multiplication equation.

Add: _____

Multiply: _____

The flour weighs _____ pounds.

Understand the Distributive Property

1 (MP) **Use Structure** Ira is making a window frame with square windowpanes. He arranges the panes in 4 rows of 6. How many windowpanes are in the arrangement?

_____

2 There are 6 rows of windows on the front of a building. There are 9 windows in each row. How many windows are on the front of the building?

_____

Use the array to complete the equations to show the Distributive Property.

3

$3 \times 8 = $ ▪

$3 \times 8 = 3 \times ($ _____ $+$ _____ $)$

$3 \times 8 = (3 \times$ _____ $) + (3 \times$ _____ $)$

$3 \times 8 = $ _____ $+$ _____

$3 \times 8 = $ _____

4

$4 \times 7 = $ ▪

$4 \times 7 = 4 \times ($ _____ $+$ _____ $)$

$4 \times 7 = (4 \times$ _____ $) + (4 \times$ _____ $)$

$4 \times 7 = $ _____ $+$ _____

$4 \times 7 = $ _____

5 **Math on the Spot** Robin says, "I can find 6×9 by multiplying 4×9 and doubling it." Does her statement make sense? Justify your answer.

_____

_____

Test Prep

6 Theo says that he painted 5 rows of 8 tiles. Select all that are equal to 5×8.

(A) $5 \times (1 + 7)$

(D) $5 \times (4 + 4)$

(B) $5 \times 3 \times 5$

(E) $3 \times 2 \times 8$

(C) $(3 + 2) \times 8$

7 An equation is shown.

$$5 \times 7 = (5 \times 4) + (5 \times \blacksquare)$$

Which is the unknown number?

(A) 1

(C) 4

(B) 3

(D) 9

8 Draw lines to match each problem on the left with the correct answer.

$6 \times (3 + 6)$ •   • 24

$(3 \times 5) + (3 \times 2)$ •   • 21

$4 \times (4 + 2)$ •   • 54

Spiral Review

9 Mariah's dog has 4 puppies. Each puppy gets a treat 10 times a week. How many treats does Mariah give the puppies each week? Complete the equation to find the number of treats.

_____ × _____ = _____ treats

10 Each bag has 7 apples. There are 6 bags. How many apples are there? Complete the equation to find the number of apples.

_____ × _____ = _____ apples

Understand the Associative Property of Multiplication

1 (MP) **Model with Mathematics** Ali makes 4 candles in one hour. She makes candles for 2 hours each day. Ali has made candles for 5 days. How many candles has Ali made in 5 days?

- Write an equation for the problem.

  _____

- Write another way to group the factors.

  _____

- How many candles has Ali made?

  _____

Show another way to group the factors. Then find the product.

2 $(7 \times 2) \times 5$ **3** $2 \times (9 \times 3)$

_____

(MP) **Reason** Write the unknown number.

4 $(4 \times 5) \times 2 = (\boxed{} \times 2) \times 4$ **5** $(7 \times 2) \times 3 = 7 \times (2 \times \boxed{})$

6 **Math on the Spot** A Kingda Ka train has 4 seats per car, but the last car has only 2 seats. How many seats are on one Kingda Ka train?

_____

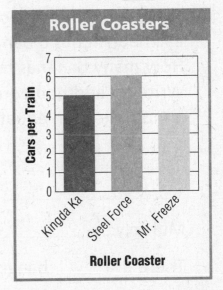

Roller Coasters

Test Prep

7 Jerry told Kalid he worked 2 hours on each of 3 days every week. He worked for 4 weeks. Kalid wrote 4 × (3 × 2). Which has the same product as 4 × (3 × 2)?

Ⓐ 2 × (4 + 3) Ⓒ (4 × 3) × 2

Ⓑ 4 × (3 × 4) Ⓓ 2 + (3 × 4)

8 An equation is shown.

(6 × 2) × 4 = 6 × (2 × ■)

Which is the unknown number?

Ⓐ 48 Ⓒ 12

Ⓑ 24 Ⓓ 4

9 Write numbers to make an equation that is true. Find the product.

(9 × 4) × 2 = ■ × (■ × ■)

_____

Spiral Review

10 There are 8 bunches of bananas. Each bunch has 6 bananas. How many bananas are there? Write an addition equation and a multiplication equation.

Add:

_____

Multiply: _____

There are _____ bananas.

11 Count to find the area of the figure. Each unit square is 1 square meter.

Area = _____ square meters

Multiply with 7

1 (MP) **Use Structure** There are 4 rows of muffins in a case. Troy puts 7 muffins in each row. How many muffins does Troy put in the case?

- Complete the array to show the problem. Draw a vertical line to break apart the array into two smaller arrays.

- Write an equation to show one way to break apart the array.

  _____

- How many muffins does Troy put in the case?

  _____

2 Complete the equations using the Commutative Property of Multiplication.

$7 \times 6 = \blacksquare$

$6 \times \underline{\hspace{1cm}} = \underline{\hspace{1cm}}$, so $7 \times \underline{\hspace{1cm}} = \underline{\hspace{1cm}}$.

Find the product.

3 $9 \times 7 = \underline{\hspace{1cm}}$

4 $\underline{\hspace{1cm}} = 7 \times 5$

5 $\begin{array}{r} 7 \\ \times\, 2 \\ \hline \end{array}$

6 $\begin{array}{r} 10 \\ \times\, 7 \\ \hline \end{array}$

7 (MP) **Reason** Explain how you can use the Commutative Property of Multiplication to find the product 7×3.

_____

_____

_____

Test Prep

8 Mr. Rios is 8×7 years old. Select all that have the same product as 8×7.

Ⓐ 7×8

Ⓑ $8 \times (3 + 4)$

Ⓒ $4 \times 4 \times 7$

Ⓓ $4 \times 2 + 7$

Ⓔ $(3 \times 7) + (5 \times 7)$

9 Find the product. $9 \times 7 = $ ▪

Ⓐ 56

Ⓑ 63

Ⓒ 79

Ⓓ 97

10 An equation is shown.

$6 \times 7 = 7 \times$ ▪

Which is the unknown number?

Ⓐ 3

Ⓑ 6

Ⓒ 7

Ⓓ 9

Spiral Review

11 Ethan arranges 6 pictures in 3 rows. What multiplication equation can you write to match the array? How many pictures are there?

_____ × _____ = _____

There are _____ pictures.

12 Find the area of the figure. Each unit square is 1 square inch. Show repeated addition. Show multiplication.

Add. _____

Multiply. _____

Area = _____ square inches

Multiply with 8

1 (MP) **Use Structure** The band members in a parade are arranged in 8 rows. There are 8 band members in each row. How many band members are in the parade?

- Break apart the array horizontally into two smaller arrays.

- Write an equation to show one way to break apart the array.

_____

- How many band members are in the parade?

_____

Write the unknown number.

2 $6 \times 8 = (6 \times 5) + (\boxed{} \times 3)$ **3** $8 \times 4 = (2 + \boxed{}) \times 4$

Find the product.

4 $8 \times 4 =$ _____   **5** $8 \times 7 =$ _____   **6** _____ $= 8 \times 5$

7 $\begin{array}{r} 8 \\ \times\, 9 \\ \hline \end{array}$ **8** $\begin{array}{r} 10 \\ \times\, 8 \\ \hline \end{array}$ **9** $\begin{array}{r} 8 \\ \times\, 8 \\ \hline \end{array}$

10 (MP) **Critique Reasoning** Jim says that if you find the product of 8 and an odd number, you can use a 4s fact and doubling to help. Is Jim correct? Explain.

_____

_____

Test Prep

11 The cashier says that the boxes of printer ink will cost 6 × $8. Select all that have the same product as 6 × 8.

Ⓐ (2 + 3) × 8   Ⓓ 6 × (5 + 3)

Ⓑ 6 × (2 × 4)   Ⓔ (6 × 7) + (6 × 1)

Ⓒ 6 × (1 + 8)

12 Find the product. 9 × 8 = ▪

Ⓐ 18   Ⓒ 72

Ⓑ 64   Ⓓ 98

13 An equation is shown.

7 × 8 = 7 × (▪ + 5)

What is the unknown number?

Ⓐ 3   Ⓒ 7

Ⓑ 5   Ⓓ 8

Spiral Review

14 Ed hangs 3 rows of pictures on a wall. There are 8 pictures in each row. How many pictures are on the wall? Write an equation that shows how Ed hangs the pictures. Then write a related fact that shows the Commutative Property of Multiplication.

_____ × _____ = _____

_____ × _____ = _____

There are _____ pictures on the wall.

15 Find the area of the figure.

3 meters

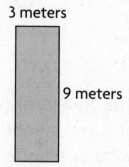

9 meters

Area = _____ square meters

LESSON 4.6
**More Practice/
Homework**

ONLINE
Ed Video Tutorials and
Interactive Examples

Multiply with 9

1 (MP) **Use Structure** A store is open 9 hours each day. It is open 6 days each week. How many hours is the store open each week? Explain how you can find the answer using the Distributive Property with multiplication and subtraction.

Monday-Saturday
9:00a.m. to 6:00p.m.
Closed on Sunday

_____

_____

_____

_____

Write the unknown number.

2 $6 \times 9 = (6 \times 10) - (6 \times \boxed{})$ **3** $7 \times 9 = 7 \times (3 + \boxed{})$

Find the product.

4 $9 \times 3 = $ _____   **5** _____ $= 7 \times 9$ **6** $\begin{array}{r} 10 \\ \times\ 9 \\ \hline \end{array}$ **7** $\begin{array}{r} 9 \\ \times\ 8 \\ \hline \end{array}$

8 **Open Ended** Al found 9×4 using $(3 + 6) \times 4$. What is another way to break apart the factor 9 to find 9×4?

_____

9 **Math on the Spot** Uranus has 27 moons. What multiplication fact with 9 can be used to find the number of moons Uranus has? Describe how you can find the fact.

_____

_____

_____

_____

Test Prep

10 Sun-Ki told Steve she rode 9 miles each day for 5 days on a bicycle trip. Select all that have the same product as 5×9.

Ⓐ $5 \times (4 + 5)$

Ⓓ $(5 \times 2) + (5 \times 7)$

Ⓑ $(5 \times 3) \times 6$

Ⓔ $9 \times (3 \times 2)$

Ⓒ $9 \times (5 + 1)$

11 An equation is shown.

$9 \times 4 = (\blacksquare + 8) \times 4$

What is the unknown number?

Ⓐ 9   Ⓑ 2   Ⓒ 1   Ⓓ 0

12 Find the product. $10 \times 9 = \blacksquare$

Ⓐ 90

Ⓒ 100

Ⓑ 99

Ⓓ 109

Spiral Review

13 Each block is 4 centimeters long. Clyde measures a book which is equal to the length of 4 blocks. What is the length of the book in centimeters?

Show the equal groups. Write a multiplication equation. Solve.

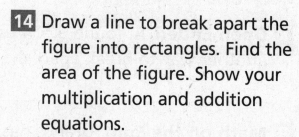

0 1 2 3 4 5 6 7 8 9 10 11 12 13 14 15 16 17

_____ × _____ = _____

The length of the book is

_____ centimeters.

14 Draw a line to break apart the figure into rectangles. Find the area of the figure. Show your multiplication and addition equations.

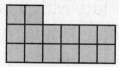

_____

Area = _____ square units

Identify Number Patterns on the Multiplication Table

1 Naomi is using the Zero Property of Multiplication to find $0 \times 6 = 0$. What is another multiplication fact that you can find using the Zero Property?

_____

2 (MP) **Use Tools** Use the multiplication table. Explain how two other columns could be used to help find the products in the 8s column.

×	0	1	2	3	4	5	6	7	8	9	10
0	0	0	0	0	0	0	0	0		0	0
1	0	1	2	3	4	5	6	7		9	10
2	0	2	4	6	8	10	12	14		18	20
3	0	3	6	9	12	15	18	21		27	30
4	0	4	8	12	16	20	24	28		36	40
5	0	5	10	15	20	25	30	35		45	50
6	0	6	12	18	24	30	36	42		54	60
7	0	7	14	21	28	35	42	49		63	70
8	0	8	16	24	32	40	48	56		72	80
9	0	9	18	27	36	45	54	63		81	90
10	0	10	20	30	40	50	60	70		90	100

_____

_____

- Complete the products in the column for the factor 8.

3 **Geography** Carl hikes the Brooke Pioneer Trail in West Virginia four days in one month. The trail is 7 miles long. How many miles does Carl hike? To find 4×7, show how you can break apart the factor 4 into equal addends.

_____

_____

Is the product even or odd? Write *even* or *odd*.

4 $2 \times 7 =$ _____

5 $5 \times 5 =$ _____

6 $9 \times 6 =$ _____

7 $10 \times 10 =$ _____

Write the unknown number.

8 $7 \times 9 = (5 + \boxed{}) \times 9$

9 $8 \times 6 = 8 \times (5 + \boxed{})$

Test Prep

10 A multiplication table is shown.

Select all the statements that correctly describe how to find the products for the factor 7.

×	0	1	2	3	4	5	6	7	8	9	10
0	0	0	0	0	0	0	0	0	0	0	0
1	0	1	2	3	4	5	6	7	8	9	10
2	0	2	4	6	8	10	12	14	16	18	20
3	0	3	6	9	12	15	18	21	24	27	30
4	0	4	8	12	16	20	24	28	32	36	40
5	0	5	10	15	20	25	30	35	40	45	50
6	0	6	12	18	24	30	36	42	48	54	60
7	0	7	14	21	28	35	42	49	56	63	70
8	0	8	16	24	32	40	48	56	64	72	80
9	0	9	18	27	36	45	54	63	72	81	90
10	0	10	20	30	40	50	60	70	80	90	100

(A) Find all the numbers that end with 7.

(B) Find all the factors that meet at a product 7.

(C) Add the products for 3 to the products for 4.

(D) Find all the numbers in the same row or the same column as the factor 7.

11 An equation is shown.

$$3 \times 8 = (\blacksquare + 2) \times 8$$

What is the unknown number? _____

Spiral Review

12 There are 3 boxes of photos on the table. There are 7 photos in each box. How many photos are in 3 boxes? Complete the bar model. Write a multiplication equation. Solve.

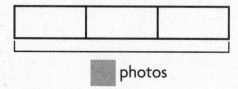

☐ photos

13 Count to find the area of the figure.

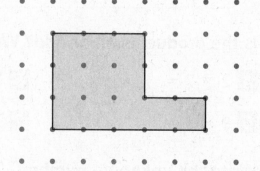

Name _____

Use the Distributive Property

1 (MP) **Critique Reasoning** Aidan says that he can use the Distributive Property to write the product 3 × 20 as 3 × (10 × 10). Is he correct? Explain your answer and complete the area model to show your reasoning.

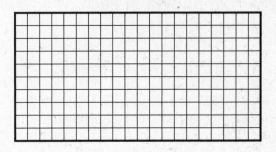

_____

_____

_____

_____

Use the Distributive Property to complete the equations. Then find the product.

2 3 × 50 = (____ × ____) + (____ × ____) + (____ × ____) + (____ × ____) + (____ × ____)

= 30 + ____ + ____ + ____ + ____

= ____

3 8 × 40 = (8 × ____) + (8 × ____) + (8 × ____) + (____ × ____)

= ____ + ____ + ____ + ____

= ____

4 **Open Ended** Write and solve a problem that involves using the Distributive Property to multiply.

_____

_____

_____

Test Prep

5 Rachel is hanging photos on a wall. She hangs 20 photos in each of 4 rows. How many photos does Rachel hang?

Ⓐ 20   Ⓑ 60   Ⓒ 80   Ⓓ 100

6 An equation is shown.

$4 \times 30 = (4 \times 10) + (4 \times 10) + (\blacksquare \times 10)$

What is the unknown number?

Ⓐ 1   Ⓑ 3   Ⓒ 4   Ⓓ 10

7 Complete the equation. Write the product.

$6 \times 40 = (6 \times 10) + (6 \times 10) + (\boxed{} \times \boxed{})$

$= \underline{}$

Spiral Review

8 Find the product. 1×10

_____

9 Use the array and the Distributive Property to complete the equation. Write the product.

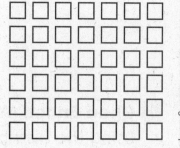

$6 \times 7 = 6 \times (\underline{} + \underline{})$

$= (6 \times \underline{}) + (6 \times \underline{})$

$= \underline{} + \underline{}$

$= \underline{}$

LESSON 5.2
**More Practice/
Homework**

ONLINE
Video Tutorials and
Interactive Examples

Use the Associative Property of Multiplication

1 (MP) **Reason** Nina rides her bike 20 miles each day for 3 days. Does Nina ride more than 75 miles? Use the Associative Property of Multiplication to explain your reasoning.

_____

_____

Write the unknown number.

2 $8 \times 40 = (8 \times \boxed{}) \times 10$ **3** $3 \times 70 = (3 \times \boxed{}) \times 10$

Show two ways to group the factors. Write the product.

4 $2 \times 50 = \underline{\quad} \times (\underline{\quad} \times \underline{\quad})$
$ = (\underline{\quad} \times \underline{\quad}) \times \underline{\quad}$
$ = \underline{\quad}$

5 $40 \times 2 = (\underline{\quad} \times \underline{\quad}) \times \underline{\quad}$
$ = \underline{\quad} \times (\underline{\quad} \times \underline{\quad})$
$ = \underline{\quad}$

6 Dustin earns $30 for each lawn he mows. How much does Dustin earn for 3 lawns?

_____

7 **Open Ended** Write a multiplication problem using 40×4, and solve your problem using the Associative Property of Multiplication and the Distributive Property.

_____

_____

Test Prep

8 Multiply 5 × 70.

(A) 35

(B) 75

(C) 280

(D) 350

9 A printer prints 30 pages in 1 minute. How many pages does the printer print in 6 minutes?

_____

10 Show two ways to group the factors. Find the product.

20 × 3 = (_____ × _____) × _____

     = _____ × (_____ × _____)

     = _____

Spiral Review

11 An equation is shown.

6 × 7 = 6 × (2 + ▪)

What is the unknown number?

_____

12 Write the unknown number.

7 × 8 = 7 × (2 × ▪)

_____

Use Place-Value Strategies to Multiply with Multiples of 10

1 (MP) **Construct Arguments** Blaise says that 4×30 is equal to 4×3 tens, or 7 tens. Is Blaise correct? Explain.

_____

_____

_____

Find the product. Use place value to find the number of tens.

2 $4 \times 60 = 4 \times$ _____ tens

= _____ tens

= _____

3 $80 \times 5 =$ _____ tens $\times$ _____

= _____ tens

= _____

4 Ricki raises money to buy supplies for her business. Each of 7 friends gives $60. How much money does Ricki raise for supplies?

_____

5 **Math on the Spot** There are 4 bottles of vitamins in each box of vitamins. Each bottle of vitamins has 30 vitamins. If the pet clinic wants to have a supply of at least 500 vitamins on hand, how many more boxes should it order?

Best Care Clinic Pet Supplies	
Item	Amount
Cat toys	10 packs
Treats	8 bags
Shampoo	20 bottles
Vitamins	3 boxes

Test Prep

6 Mr. Han gives 20 counters to each of 5 students. How many counters does Mr. Han give out?

  (A) 25

  (B) 100

  (C) 250

  (D) 1,000

7 Jocelyn practices playing the violin 7 days a week. Each practice session is 30 minutes long. How many minutes does Jocelyn practice each week?

_____

8 Sanjay is trying to finish a book that has 360 pages. He reads 40 pages each day. Can Sanjay finish his book in 8 days? Explain.

_____

9 Rini says that the product 6×40 is equal to the product 3×80. Is she correct? Use place value to explain your answer.

_____

_____

Spiral Review

10 Show another way to group the factors. Then find the product.

$(7 \times 2) \times 5$

_____

11 Find the product.

_____ $= 6 \times 8$

© Houghton Mifflin Harcourt Publishing Company

LESSON 5.4
**More Practice/
Homework**

ONLINE
Video Tutorials and
Interactive Examples

Multiply Multiples of 10 by 1-Digit Numbers

1 (MP) **Use Structure** Mrs. Jackson buys 6 packages of paper plates for the school picnic. Each package has 40 plates. How many plates does she buy? Show your work.

_____

_____

_____

Find the product.

2 $5 \times 40 =$ _____

3 $7 \times 60 =$ _____

4 _____ $= 8 \times 30$

5
$$\begin{array}{r} 90 \\ \times\ 6 \\ \hline \end{array}$$

6
$$\begin{array}{r} 50 \\ \times\ 3 \\ \hline \end{array}$$

7
$$\begin{array}{r} 70 \\ \times\ 2 \\ \hline \end{array}$$

8 Aisha is packing cans of food into boxes like this. Aisha has 9 boxes. How many cans of food can Aisha pack?

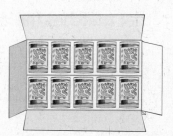

_____

9 **Math on the Spot** Ava's class buys 8 packages of balloons for the class celebration. Each package has 50 balloons. If 21 balloons are left over, how many balloons are used for the party?

_____

Test Prep

10 Celia rides her bicycle for 2 hours every day. How many hours does she ride in 30 days?

(A) 60 hours

(B) 90 hours

(C) 120 hours

(D) 600 hours

11 Omar has 7 bags of marbles. Each bag holds 30 marbles. How many marbles does Omar have?

_____

12 What is the product of 8 and 40?

_____

13 Find the product.

$$\begin{array}{r} 90 \\ \times\ 7 \\ \hline \end{array}$$

14 Write and solve a problem that matches the drawing.

_____

_____

_____

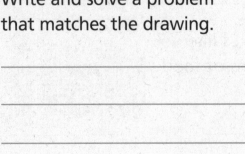
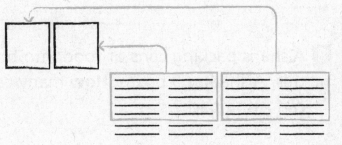

© Houghton Mifflin Harcourt Publishing Company

Spiral Review

15 Write the unknown number.

$6 \times 9 = (6 \times 5) + (6 \times \underline{\quad})$

16 Find the product. 8×8

_____

Name _____

Represent Division

1 (MP) **Use Tools** Charles is going on a hiking trip. He will hike 32 miles on the trip. He plans to hike the same number of miles each day. He will hike for 4 days. How many miles will Charles hike each day?

- Draw to show equal groups.

- How many miles will Charles hike each day?

_____

2 Leann has 48 straws to build figures. She uses 6 straws to make each figure. How many figures does Leann make?

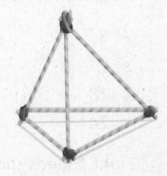

_____

3 **Math on the Spot** At Luke's school party, the children get into teams of 6 to play a game. If there are 30 boys and 24 girls, how many teams are there?

_____

4 **Open Ended** Choose any package of items from the table. Write a word problem about equally sharing the items in the package.

Mill Town Craft Supplies	
Item	Number in Each Package
Craft Sticks	28
Beads	42
Straws	32

_____

_____

_____

Test Prep

5 Rosia has 80 sheets of paper. She separates the sheets into 10 equal groups. How many sheets are in each group?

Ⓐ 8

Ⓑ 10

Ⓒ 70

Ⓓ 90

6 Don is making jump ropes. He has 21 feet of rope. He cuts the rope to make jump ropes that are each 7 feet long. How many jump ropes does he make?

Ⓐ 3

Ⓑ 7

Ⓒ 18

Ⓓ 24

7 Eight friends share 32 apples. Each friend gets the same number of apples. How many apples does each friend get?

- Show the number of apples in each group.

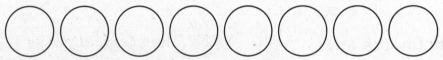

- How many apples does each friend get?

_____

Spiral Review

Find the product.

8 6 × 8 = _____   **9** 9 × 4 = _____

LESSON 6.2
**More Practice/
Homework**

ONLINE
Video Tutorials and
Interactive Examples

Separate Objects into Equal Groups

1 (MP) **Use Tools** Dori works at a flower shop. She has 24 flowers and 4 vases. She places an equal number of flowers in each vase. How many flowers are in each vase?

• Draw to show equal groups.

• How many flowers are in each vase?

_____

2 Jimmy puts 60 shirts on 6 shelves at the store. Each shelf has the same number of shirts. How many shirts are on each shelf?

_____

3 **Math on the Spot** Joe and Ella combine their photos. Then they put an equal number on each page of an 8-page photo album. How many photos are on each page?

Photos	
Name	**Number of Photos**
Madison	28
Joe	25
Ella	15

4 (MP) **Construct Arguments** Raul finds a way to divide 48 building blocks into 6 equal groups. Jerry finds a way to divide 48 building blocks into 8 equal groups. Whose way has the greater number of building blocks in each group? Explain.

_____

_____

_____

Test Prep

5 Harold packs 36 books into 4 boxes. He puts an equal number of books in each box. How many books are in each box?

- (A) 6
- (B) 9
- (C) 32
- (D) 40

6 Nine art students equally share 63 crayons. How many crayons does each art student get? Select all the sentences that are true.

- (A) There are 7 equal groups.
- (B) There are 9 equal groups.
- (C) There are 7 crayons in each group.
- (D) There are 9 crayons in each group.
- (E) There are 63 crayons in each group.

7 If 64 bagels are divided among 8 bags, how many bagels are in each bag?

_____

Spiral Review

8 Find the product.

$9 \times 9 =$ _____

9 How can you break apart the factor 4 into equal addends to find the product 4×7?

_____

_____

© Houghton Mifflin Harcourt Publishing Company

Find the Number of Equal Groups

1 (MP) **Use Tools** Yolanda needs 32 screws to make wooden benches. She uses 4 screws to make each bench. How many benches can she make?

- Draw to show equal groups.

- How many benches can Yolanda make?

_____

2 A grocery store has a display of 64 pears. Casey packs 8 pears in each bag. How many bags does Casey fill?

_____

3 **Math on the Spot** A store has 22 red beach balls and 18 green beach balls in boxes of 5 beach balls each. How many boxes of beach balls are at the store?

_____

4 (MP) **Use Structure** Find four different ways that 12 objects can be put into equal groups. Describe your method for finding the equal groups.

_____

_____

_____

_____

Test Prep

5 Gaby cuts 45 tomato slices. She puts 5 tomato slices on each salad plate. How many salad plates can she make?

- (A) 50
- (B) 40
- (C) 9
- (D) 8

6 Russ collects 30 eggs from a chicken coop. He puts 6 eggs in each carton. How many cartons of eggs does he fill? Which sentence is true?

- (A) Russ fills 5 cartons of eggs.
- (B) Russ fills 6 cartons of eggs.
- (C) There are 5 eggs in each group.
- (D) The total number of eggs is 36.

7 If 64 jars of fruit jam are placed in equal groups of 8 on a shelf, how many shelves are filled?

_____

Spiral Review

8 Lupe says that the product of 4 and any number is even. Does her statement make sense? Explain.

_____

_____

9 A copier makes 80 copies in a minute. How many copies can the copier make in 7 minutes? Write an equation that solves the problem.

_____

_____

Relate Subtraction and Division

1 (MP) **Reason** Carmen buys 27 pounds of hay for her rabbits. Each bag weighs 9 pounds. How many bags of hay does Carmen buy?

Hay
9 pounds

- Show your work.

- How many bags of hay does Carmen buy?

_____

2 A library has 42 storybooks. Vito puts the same number of storybooks on each shelf. He fills 6 shelves. How many storybooks are on each shelf?

_____

3 **Math on the Spot** Dwayne brought an equal number of box tops to school each day for 5 days. Alma also brought an equal number of box tops each day for 5 days. How many box tops did the two students bring in altogether each day? Explain.

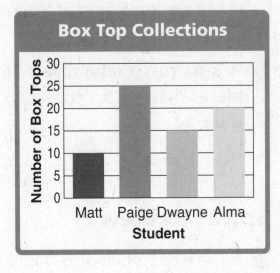

Box Top Collections

_____

_____

_____

4 (MP) **Model with Mathematics** Lili has 28 walnuts. She puts 7 walnuts in each package. How many packages of walnuts does Lili make? Write different equations that can be used to model and solve the problem.

_____

Test Prep

5 Ms. Tran has 32 jars of paint. She separates the jars of paint into 8 equal groups. How many jars of paint are in each group?

(A) 3

(C) 24

(B) 4

(D) 40

6 Erik makes 30 animal figures. He puts 6 animal figures on each shelf. How many shelves does Erik fill? Select all the sentences that match the information.

(A) Erik fills 5 shelves.

(D) There are 6 animal figures in each group.

(B) Erik fills 6 shelves.

(E) There are 30 animal figures in each group.

(C) There are 5 animal figures in each group.

7 If Tessa cuts a rope that is 36 inches long into equal pieces that are 6 inches long, how many pieces does she cut?

_____

Spiral Review

8 A store has 5 boxes of trading cards on display. Each box has 80 trading cards. How many trading cards are on display?

_____

9 Ester writes 6 × 7 = 42 to find the number of students seated at tables. Describe what each factor represents.

_____

_____

_____

Represent Division with Arrays

1 (MP) **Use Tools** Albert makes an array with 24 tiles. He puts 6 tiles in each row. How many rows are there?

• Draw an array.

• Write a division equation to find how many rows of tiles there are.

_____

2 Tami has 36 number cards. She places the cards into 9 equal rows. How many cards are in each row?

_____

3 **Math on the Spot** Tell how to use an array to find how many rows of 9 are in 63.

_____

_____

_____

4 (MP) **Model with Mathematics** Marcello arranges 35 index cards into 7 equal rows. How many index cards are in each row? Write a division equation to model the problem.

_____

Test Prep

5 Riley uses 54 cloth squares to make a quilt. She puts the cloth squares into equal rows with 9 cloth squares in each row. How many rows does she make?

(A) 6   (B) 9   (C) 45   (D) 63

6 Jamar packs 48 mugs into a box. He puts the mugs into 6 equal rows. How many mugs are in each row? Which sentence is true?

(A) Jamar makes 8 rows.

(B) There are 8 mugs in each row.

(C) There are 6 mugs in each row.

(D) There are 42 mugs in each row.

7 Francie arranges 56 counters into 7 equal rows. How many counters are in each row?

_____

Spiral Review

8 Use the Associative Property of Multiplication to find the product.

$2 \times 30 =$ ▪

_____

_____

9 A closet has a tiled floor. Each tile is 1 square foot. What is the area of the closet floor?

Name _____

LESSON 6.6
More Practice/ Homework

ONLINE
Video Tutorials and
Interactive Examples

Represent Division with Bar Models

1 (MP) **Use Tools** Dori puts 72 pounds of wood boards in a wheelbarrow. Each wood board weighs 8 pounds. How many wood boards are there?

■ wood boards

72 pounds

- Complete the bar model to show the problem.

- Write a division equation. How many wood boards are there?

_____

2 (MP) **Reason** Yazmin has a package of 36 crackers. She shares the crackers equally among eight friends and herself. How many crackers does each person get?

_____

3 **Math on the Spot** Kevin bought a box of Puppy Chips for his dog. If he gives his small dog 2 treats each day and his big dog 3 treats each day, for how many days will one box of treats last?

Dog Treats	
Type	Number in Box
Chew Sticks	12
Chewies	20
Dog Bites	30
Puppy Chips	40

_____

4 (MP) **Model with Mathematics** If 30 pencils are shared equally among 10 students, how many pencils does each student get? Write a division equation to model the problem. Then solve.

_____

Test Prep

5 Ernie has 14 markers and 2 boxes. He places an equal number of markers in each box. How many markers are in each box?

Ⓐ 16

Ⓑ 12

Ⓒ 8

Ⓓ 7

6 Sofia has 63 leaves in her collection. She puts 9 leaves on each page of her book until there are no leaves left. How many pages does she fill?

Ⓐ 7   Ⓒ 54

Ⓑ 8   Ⓓ 72

7 Danny gives an equal number of baseball cards to each friend. He gives 36 ÷ 4 baseball cards to each friend. Describe how many baseball cards there are and how many cards each friend gets.

_____

_____

Spiral Review

8 Use place value to find the product.

$8 \times 60 = 8 \times$ _____ tens

$=$ _____ tens

$=$ _____

9 Jack has a tank for his lizard. The tank floor is in the shape of a rectangle. One side of the rectangle is 2 feet long. Another side is 3 feet long. What is the area of the floor of the tank?

_____

Name _____

LESSON 6.7
**More Practice/
Homework**

⊙Ed **ONLINE**
Video Tutorials and
Interactive Examples

Apply Division Rules for 1 and 0

1 (MP) **Use Structure** There are 0 riders and 4 rowboats. How many riders are in each rowboat?

- Draw to show equal groups.

- Write a division equation.

_____

- How many riders are in each rowboat?

_____

2 There are 7 pumpkins and 7 friends. The friends will equally share the pumpkins. How many pumpkins does each friend get? Write a division equation.

_____

Divide. Find the quotient.

3 _____ = 3 ÷ 3   **4** 9 ÷ 1 = _____   **5** $7\overline{)0}$

6 **Math on the Spot** Claire has 6 parakeets. She puts 4 of them in a cage. She divides the other parakeets equally among 2 friends to hold. How many parakeets does each friend get to hold?

7 (MP) **Critique Reasoning** Dean says that when you divide a number by 0, the quotient is always 0. Is Dean correct? Explain.

_____

_____

_____

Test Prep

8 There are 9 peaches and 9 friends. The friends share the peaches equally. How many peaches does each friend get?

(A) 0

(B) 1

(C) 9

(D) 18

9 What is the unknown number in this equation?

$7 \div 1 = \blacksquare$

(A) 0

(C) 6

(B) 1

(D) 7

10 Select all the facts that have a quotient of 0.

(A) $0 \div 1$

(B) $1 \div 1$

(C) $0 \div 8$

(D) $8 \div 1$

(E) $0 \div 9$

Spiral Review

11 Find the product.

$4 \times 70 =$ _____

12 Jaime is making tacos for her family. Each person eats 2 tacos. There are 6 people in her family. How many tacos does Jaime make?

_____

Name _____

LESSON 7.1
**More Practice/
Homework**

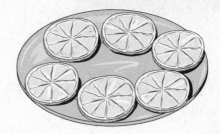

ONLINE
Video Tutorials and
Interactive Examples

Relate Multiplication and Division

1 (MP) **Model with Mathematics** Marko has 24 orange slices. He puts groups of 6 orange slices on each plate. Write a multiplication equation and a division equation to find how many plates Marko needs.

_____

(MP) **Use Tools** Use the visual model to complete the equations.

2

18

18 ÷ 6 = _____

6 × _____ = 18

3
● ● ● ● ●
● ● ● ● ●

10 ÷ 2 = _____

2 × _____ = 10

(MP) **Use Structure** Write the unknown number.

4 $4)\overline{20}$

4 × ■ = 20

■ = _____

5 ■ × 3 = 27

27 ÷ 3 = ■

■ = _____

6 16 ÷ ■ = 8

■ × 8 = 16

■ = _____

7 **Math on the Spot** Garrett is 8 years old. He and his family are going to the county fair. What is the price of admission for Garrett, his 2 parents, his grandmother, and his baby sister?

Cochise County Fair	
Price of Admission	
Adults	$5
Students	$3
Children 5 and under free	

_____

© Houghton Mifflin Harcourt Publishing Company

Module 7 • Lesson 1

P65

Test Prep

8 Write a multiplication equation that could be used to solve $18 \div 2 = \blacksquare$.

_____

9 Write a division equation that could be used to solve $4 \times \blacksquare = 28$.

_____

10 Select all the equations that can be used to solve $36 \div 9 = \blacksquare$.

(A) $36 \times 9 = \blacksquare$

(B) $9 \times \blacksquare = 36$

(C) $\blacksquare \times 9 = 36$

(D) $\blacksquare \div 9 = 36$

(E) $36 \div \blacksquare = 9$

11 There are 24 students in the library. The students are sitting in equal groups at 6 tables. How many students are in each group? Write an equation to model and solve the problem.

_____

Spiral Review

12 Shana makes seashell necklaces. She has a piece of string that is 64 inches long. Each necklace is 8 inches long. How many necklaces can Shana make?

13 Jake and his 4 friends equally share 45 marbles to play a game. How many marbles does each person get?

_____

Write Related Facts

1 (MP) **Model with Mathematics** There are 6 vases. Each vase has the number of flowers shown. What multiplication equation represents the number of flowers? Write a related division equation.

_____

_____

Write the related facts for the set of numbers.

2 4, 5, 20

_____ ÷ _____ = _____

_____ × _____ = _____

_____ ÷ _____ = _____

_____ × _____ = _____

3 3, 6, 18

_____ ÷ _____ = _____

_____ × _____ = _____

_____ ÷ _____ = _____

_____ × _____ = _____

(MP) **Use Structure** Complete the related facts.

4 5 × _____ = 40

_____ × 5 = 40

40 ÷ _____ = 5

40 ÷ 5 = _____

5 _____ × 7 = 42

7 × _____ = 42

42 ÷ 7 = _____

42 ÷ _____ = 7

6 **Math on the Spot** Mr. Lee divides 2 packages of clay and 1 package of glitter dough equally among 4 students. How many more glitter dough sections than clay sections does each student get?

Clay Supplies	
Item	Number in Package
Clay	12 sections
Clay tool set	11 tools
Glitter dough	36 sections

_____

Test Prep

7 Which is a related fact for the set of numbers 4, 8, 32?

Ⓐ $4 \times 2 = 8$

Ⓑ $32 - 8 = 24$

Ⓒ $4 \times 8 = 32$

Ⓓ $8 \div 4 = 2$

8 Complete the related facts.

$5 \times \blacksquare = 45$

$45 \div \blacksquare = 5$

$\blacksquare = $ _____

9 Select all the related facts for 3, 7, 21.

Ⓐ $3 \times 7 = 21$

Ⓑ $21 - 7 = 14$

Ⓒ $21 + 7 = 28$

Ⓓ $21 \div 7 = 3$

Ⓔ $7 \times 3 = 21$

Ⓕ $21 \div 3 = 7$

Spiral Review

10 A store has 36 ties and 6 racks to hang the ties. Jonah places the same number of ties on each rack. How many ties does Jonah place on each rack?

11 Marc is making jackets. He has 48 buttons. He sews 8 buttons onto each jacket. How many jackets can Marc make?

Multiply and Divide with 2, 4, and 8

1 (MP) **Model with Mathematics** Maya packs 48 stuffed animals. She packs 8 stuffed animals in each box. How many boxes of stuffed animals does Maya pack? Write an equation to model the problem.

_____

_____

(MP) **Use Repeated Reasoning** Multiply or divide.

2 $8 \times 7 =$ _____ **3** $5\overline{)20}$ **4** $2\overline{)20}$

5 $18 \div 9 =$ _____ **6** _____ $= 4 \times 6$ **7** $4 \div 4 =$ _____

8 $\begin{array}{r} 2 \\ \times 7 \\ \hline \end{array}$ **9** $\begin{array}{r} 8 \\ \times 4 \\ \hline \end{array}$ **10** $\begin{array}{r} 9 \\ \times 8 \\ \hline \end{array}$ **11** $\begin{array}{r} 3 \\ \times 4 \\ \hline \end{array}$

12 **Math on the Spot** There are 34 people camping at Max's family reunion. They have cabin tents and vista tents. How many of each type of tent do they need to sleep exactly 34 people if each tent is filled? Explain.

Tent Sizes	
Type	**Number of People**
Cabin	10
Vista	8

_____

_____

_____

Test Prep

13 Multiply 4 × 9.

- Ⓐ 5
- Ⓑ 13
- Ⓒ 32
- Ⓓ 36

14 Divide 56 ÷ 8.

- Ⓐ 7
- Ⓑ 9
- Ⓒ 48
- Ⓓ 64

15 Multiply 2 × 8.

_____

16 Divide 16 ÷ 4.

_____

17 What number multiplied by 4 equals 32?

_____

Spiral Review

18 Jessa has 14 roses. She puts 2 roses in each flower arrangement that she is making. How many flower arrangements can Jessa make?

19 A pitcher has 4 cups of lemonade. Reggie drinks 1 cup each morning. How many days will the lemonade last?

LESSON 7.4
**More Practice/
Homework**

Ed **ONLINE**
Video Tutorials and
Interactive Examples

Multiply and Divide with 5 and 10

1 (MP) **Use Structure** How can you use a multiplication fact to find $30 \div 5$?

_____

_____

_____

(MP) **Use Structure** Complete the related facts.

2 $5 \times$ _____ $= 45$ **3** $60 \div$ _____ $= 6$ **4** $35 \div$ _____ $= 7$

$45 \div 5 =$ _____ $6 \times$ _____ $= 60$ $7 \times$ _____ $= 35$

(MP) **Use Repeated Reasoning** Multiply or divide.

5 $15 \div 5 =$ _____   **6** $10 \times 8 =$ _____   **7** $5 \overline{)25}$

8 Reuben has 70 feet of rope. He cuts the rope into 10 equal pieces. How long is each piece of rope?

_____

9 **Math on the Spot** Lena wants to put the elephant stickers in an album. She says she will use more pages if she puts 5 stickers on a page instead of 10 stickers on a page. Is she correct? Explain.

Animal Stickers					
Elephants	☐	☐	☐	☐	☐
Giraffes	☐	☐	☐		
Monkeys	☐	☐	☐	☐	

Key: Each ☐ = 10 stickers.

_____

_____

_____

Test Prep

10 Multiply 5 × 7.

  (A) 2
  (B) 12
  (C) 30
  (D) 35

11 Divide 90 ÷ 10.

  (A) 8
  (B) 9
  (C) 80
  (D) 100

12 Multiply 4 × 5.

  _____

13 Divide 50 ÷ 10.

  _____

14 Multiply 10 × 10.

  _____

Spiral Review

15 Mr. Landry has 12 feet of rope, which he cuts into 4 equal pieces. How long is each piece of rope?

16 Micah draws a design of a house with 14 windows on the front. There are 7 windows in a row on each floor. How many rows of windows does Micah's design have?

Multiply and Divide with 3 and 6

ONLINE
Ed
Video Tutorials and
Interactive Examples

1 (MP) **Reason** Li rides his bicycle 60 miles each week to train for a race. He rides 6 days a week. The answer to this problem is 10 miles. Write a question for this problem.

_____

_____

(MP) **Use Repeated Reasoning** Find the product.

2 $3 \times 7 =$ _____   **3** $4 \times 6 =$ _____   **4** _____ $= 9 \times 3$

(MP) **Use Repeated Reasoning** Find the quotient.

5 $15 \div 3 =$ _____   **6** $60 \div 6 =$ _____   **7** $6\overline{)30}$

8 There are 42 cans of soup on a shelf. Brandon can fit 6 cans in a box. How many boxes can Brandon fill?

_____

9 Sonya buys some apples. What is the cost of 10 pounds of apples?

_____

Apples
$3 per pound

10 **Math on the Spot** Students doing the jump-rope race and the beanbag toss compete in teams of 3. How many more teams participate in the jump-rope race than in the beanbag toss? Explain how you know.

Field Day Events	
Activity	Number of Students
Beanbag toss	21
Jump-rope race	27

_____

Test Prep

11 Multiply 6 × 3.

- (A) 2
- (B) 3
- (C) 12
- (D) 18

12 Divide 42 ÷ 6.

- (A) 7
- (B) 8
- (C) 36
- (D) 48

13 Select all the equations with an unknown factor of 3.

- (A) ■ × 5 = 15
- (B) 9 × ■ = 54
- (C) ■ × 4 = 24
- (D) ■ × 7 = 21
- (E) 6 × ■ = 18

14 Divide 24 ÷ 3.

_____

Spiral Review

15 The seats in the theater are arranged in rows. There are 72 seats in each section and 9 seats in each row. How many rows are in each section of the theater?

16 Jordan has a pack of baseball cards. There are 32 cards in the pack. Jordan shares them equally among 4 friends. How many cards does each friend get?

LESSON 7.6
**More Practice/
Homework**

ONLINE
Video Tutorials and
Interactive Examples

Multiply and Divide
with 7 and 9

1 (MP) **Use Structure** Explain how you could
break apart this array to find 7×8.

_____

_____

_____

_____

(MP) **Use Repeated Reasoning** Find the product.

2 $5 \times 9 =$ _____   **3** _____ $= 7 \times 4$ **4** $9 \times 9 =$ _____

(MP) **Use Repeated Reasoning** Find the quotient.

5 $63 \div 7 =$ _____   **6** $27 \div 9 =$ _____   **7** $7\overline{)49}$

8 Diana has 42 inches of fabric. She cuts the fabric into
7 equal pieces. How long is each piece?

_____

9 Oscar shares 38 red marbles and 34 blue marbles
among his friends. Each friend gets 9 marbles. How
many friends get marbles?

_____

10 **Math on the Spot** Gavin sold 21 bagels to 7 different
people. Each person bought the same number of bagels.
How many bagels did Gavin sell to each person? Explain.

_____

_____

_____

Test Prep

11 An equation is shown.

$$9 \times 5 = \blacksquare \times 9$$

What is the unknown number?

Ⓐ 4

Ⓑ 5

Ⓒ 14

Ⓓ 45

12 Divide $28 \div 7$.

Ⓐ 4

Ⓑ 5

Ⓒ 21

Ⓓ 35

13 Select all that could be used to find 8×7.

Ⓐ 7×8

Ⓑ $8 \times (5 + 2)$

Ⓒ $8 + (5 + 2)$

Ⓓ $(8 \times 3) + (8 \times 4)$

Ⓔ $(8 \times 3) \times (8 \times 4)$

Spiral Review

14 Alfie has 9 books. He puts 1 book on each shelf of a bookcase. How many shelves does the bookcase have?

15 Andy stacks 6 nickels. What is the value of Andy's nickels?

Build Fluency with Multiplication and Division

1 (MP) **Model with Mathematics** There are 63 students cleaning a playground. Each group has 9 students. How many groups of students are cleaning the playground?

- Write a multiplication equation and a division equation to model the problem.

_____

- How many groups of students are cleaning the playground?

_____

(MP) **Use Structure** Complete the related facts.

2 $6 \times$ _____ $= 42$

$42 \div 6 =$ _____

3 $3 \times$ _____ $= 24$

$24 \div$ _____ $= 3$

4 _____ $\times 2 = 18$

$18 \div$ _____ $= 2$

(MP) **Use Repeated Reasoning** Multiply or divide.

5 $5 \times 8 =$ _____

6 $4\overline{)36}$

7 _____ $= 56 \div 7$

8 $40 \div 4 =$ _____

9 $7 \times 7 =$ _____

10 $4\overline{)20}$

11 _____ $= 3 \times 9$

12 $9\overline{)54}$

13 $4 \div 4 =$ _____

14 There are 80 chairs in a school music room arranged in equal rows of 8. How many rows of chairs are there?

_____

Test Prep

15 Which equation related to $24 \div 6 = \blacksquare$ can be used to solve the division problem?

(A) $4 \times 2 = 8$

(B) $6 \times 4 = 24$

(C) $2 \times 8 = 16$

(D) $24 + 6 = 30$

16 Multiply 3×9.

(A) 3

(B) 6

(C) 12

(D) 27

17 Multiply 8×8.

_____

18 Divide $40 \div 4$.

_____

19 Brit counts 5 petals on each flower. There are 7 flowers. How many petals does Brit count?

_____

Spiral Review

20 Sonja makes a design with 3 rows of stickers. There are 5 stickers in each row. How many stickers are in Sonja's design?

21 There are 5 boxes in the storage room. Each box has 0 objects. How many objects are in the boxes?

LESSON 8.1
**More Practice/
Homework**

Ed **ONLINE**
Video Tutorials and
Interactive Examples

Identify and Extend Patterns

1 **(MP) Use Structure** There are 7 days in a week.
If Maria needs to plan 1 activity every day for the next
3 weeks, how many activities does Maria need to plan?

_____

(MP) Use Structure Describe a pattern. Then write a rule and
extend your pattern.

2 12 20 28 36 _____

Rule: _____

3 14 34 54 74 94 _____

Rule: _____

4 3 6 9 12 _____

Rule: _____

5 10 20 30 40 _____

Rule: _____

6 **Math on the Spot** Students made
a craft project at camp. They used
4 small pine cone patterns and 3 large
pine cone patterns. Complete the
table to find how many patterns
were used for the different numbers
of projects.

Projects	1	2	3	4	5	6	7	8	9	10
Small Pattern	4									
Large Pattern	3									

7 Every clownfish in the aquarium has 3 stripes. How
many stripes do 8 clownfish in the aquarium have?

_____

Test Prep

8 Marla is setting the table. Each place setting has 3 different-sized dishes. If 6 people will be eating dinner, how many dishes does Marla need?

  (A) 9   (C) 18

  (B) 12   (D) 21

9 Which number completes the pattern in the table?

Bears	1	2	3	4	5
Paws	4	8	12	16	

  (A) 27

  (B) 22

  (C) 20

  (D) 17

10 This pattern is written on the board:

7 13 19 25 31

Jenny says the next number in the pattern is 38. What mistake does Jenny make?

_____

Spiral Review

11 Write the unknown number.

$$6)\overline{42}$$

$6 \times \blacksquare = 42$

$\blacksquare = \underline{\hspace{1cm}}$

12 Write the unknown number.

$$4 \times 9 = 4 \times (4 + \boxed{})$$

© Houghton Mifflin Harcourt Publishing Company

Name _____

LESSON 8.2
More Practice/ Homework

ONLINE
Video Tutorials and
Interactive Examples

Find Unknown Factors and Numbers

Write a multiplication equation and a division equation with an unknown. Solve.

1 **Language Arts** Jonas uses features like maps, photographs, and captions to help understand the non-fiction book he is reading. On the first 5 pages of the book, Jonas sees 20 photographs with captions. If each page has the same number of photographs, how many photographs are on each page?

2 (MP) **Model with Mathematics** Mia practices the piano for 8 hours this week. She practices for the same number of hours each day for 4 days. How many hours does she practice each day?

3 (MP) **Model with Mathematics** Ely mows lawns for 12 hours on Saturday and Sunday. He spends 2 hours mowing each lawn. How many lawns does he mow on Saturday and Sunday?

Find the unknown number.

4 $16 \div \boxed{} = 4$ **5** $\boxed{} \div 8 = 4$ **6** $18 = 2 \times \boxed{}$

7 $6 \times \boxed{} = 30$ **8** $7 = 42 \div \boxed{}$ **9** $54 \div \boxed{} = 6$

10 $\boxed{} \times 8 = 24$ **11** $48 = \boxed{} \times 6$ **12** $\boxed{} \div 3 = 9$

Test Prep

13 Which is the value of the unknown number in the equation $20 \div \blacksquare = 2$?

- (A) 40
- (B) 18
- (C) 12
- (D) 10

14 A division problem is shown.

$$24 \div \blacksquare = 4$$

Which is a related equation that could be used to solve the division problem?

- (A) $8 \times 3 = 24$
- (B) $4 \times 6 = 24$
- (C) $3 \times 8 = 24$
- (D) $4 + 20 = 24$

15 What is the value of the unknown number in the equation $\blacksquare \times 9 = 63$?

_____

Spiral Review

16 Multiply.

$$8 \times 3 = \text{_____}$$

17 Show another way to group the factors. Then find the product.

$$4 \times (2 \times 3)$$

_____

LESSON 8.3
**More Practice/
Homework**

Ed **ONLINE**
Video Tutorials and
Interactive Examples

Use Multiplication and Division to Solve Problem Situations

Write an equation. Use the letter *n* for the unknown number. Solve.

1 (MP) **Model with Mathematics** Ella has 64 inches of ribbon to make necklaces. She uses 8 inches of ribbon for each necklace. How many necklaces can Ella make?

_____

n = _____

2 (MP) **Model with Mathematics** Cooper plants 36 tomato plants in 4 rows in a garden. Each row has the same number of plants. How many tomato plants are in each row?

_____

n = _____

3 (MP) **Model with Mathematics** Ms. Jay walks 35 miles each week to deliver mail. She walks 5 days each week and walks the same number of miles each day. How many miles does Ms. Jay walk each day?

Multiplication equation: _____

Division equation: _____

n = _____

Find the value of the unknown number.

4 $6 \times s = 24$

s = _____

5 $v \div 7 = 8$

v = _____

6 $27 = z \times 3$

z = _____

Test Prep

7 Jenna places 72 books onto 8 shelves of a bookshelf. She places the same number of books on each shelf. Select all the equations that could represent how to find the number of books on each shelf.

(A) $72 \times 8 = n$

(B) $8 \times n = 72$

(C) $72 - 8 = n$

(D) $72 \times n = 8$

(E) $72 \div 8 = n$

8 Amira is organizing paint supplies. She puts 32 paint bottles into 4 rows. Each row has the same number of paint bottles. How many paint bottles does she put in each row?

(A) 28

(B) 9

(C) 8

(D) 6

9 There are 45 bags of dog food in 5 boxes at the pet store. Each box has the same number of bags. How many bags of dog food are in each box?

(A) 7

(B) 9

(C) 40

(D) 50

Spiral Review

10 Multiply or divide.

$4 \times 3 = $ _____

$40 \div 5 = $ _____

11 Write the unknown factor.

$9 \times 3 = \boxed{} \times 9$

Solve Two-Step Problems

(MP) **Model with Mathematics** Write two equations with letters for the unknowns. Solve. You can use a visual model to help.

1 Gemma has 3 rose bushes, each with the same number of roses. She picks 4 of the roses. There are 20 roses left on the rose bushes. How many roses were on each rose bush?

_____

_____

2 Brianna cuts a piece of yarn into 4 equal-length pieces. Then she cuts 2 inches off one of the pieces, leaving 5 inches of yarn on the piece. What was the length of the original piece of yarn?

_____

_____

3 Milo has 5 rocks in his rock collection. He finds 40 rocks outside that he wants to put in his collection. If he places the rocks into boxes of 9, how many boxes of rocks will he have in his collection?

_____

_____

4 In the mountains, Mrs. Flores can rent a campsite for $9 each day, plus a one-time fee of $25. She rents a campsite for 4 days. How much does it cost Mrs. Flores to rent the campsite?

_____

_____

Test Prep

5 Shia has 6 new boxes of crayons. Each box has 8 crayons. He also has 7 crayons from an old box. How many crayons does he have?

Ⓐ 21

Ⓑ 42

Ⓒ 48

Ⓓ 55

6 Kira has 3 shelves of books. Each shelf has 4 books. She also has 5 books that are not on shelves. How many books does she have? Write two equations with letters for the unknowns. Solve.

_____

7 Vera cut a piece of fabric into 5 equal-length pieces. Then she cut another 3 centimeters off one piece, leaving 6 centimeters of fabric. How many centimeters long was her original piece of fabric? Write two equations with letters for the unknowns. Solve.

_____

_____

Spiral Review

8 Ricky has 14 inches of tape. He cuts the tape into 2-inch pieces. How many pieces of tape does Ricky have?

_____

9 Multiply.

$8 \times 3 =$ _____

$8 \times 5 =$ _____

© Houghton Mifflin Harcourt Publishing Company

LESSON 8.5
**More Practice/
Homework**

ONLINE
Video Tutorials and
Interactive Examples

Practice with One- and Two-Step Problems

(MP) **Model with Mathematics** Write equations. Use letters for the unknowns. Solve.

1 A builder has a piece of wood that is 27 inches long. He cuts the wood into 3 equal-length pieces. Then he cuts some inches off one of the pieces, leaving 4 inches. How many inches of wood does he cut off of one of the pieces?

2 Jai paddles 8 miles on a kayak each day for 4 days. On the fifth day, he paddles some more miles. In 5 days, he paddles 40 miles. How many miles does he paddle on the kayak on the fifth day?

3 Oak trees are planted in 4 rows at the park. Each row has the same number of trees. If 36 oak trees are planted, how many trees are there in each row?

4 Mya has 4 baskets of flowers. Each basket has the same number of flowers. She also has 3 single flowers. If Mya has 43 flowers, how many flowers are in each basket?

Test Prep

5 Amy is setting up chairs for the band concert. She places 48 chairs in 6 rows. Each row has the same number of chairs. How many chairs are in each row?

(A) 42

(C) 8

(B) 14

(D) 6

6 Gia spends $54 at the store on groceries. She also buys a toothbrush and toothpaste that each cost $5. How much money does Gia spend?

(A) $49

(C) $59

(B) $55

(D) $64

7 One section of the stadium has 6 rows. Each row has 7 seats. If 8 seats are reserved, how many seats are not reserved?

(A) 34

(C) 50

(B) 42

(D) 56

Spiral Review

8 Find the quotient.

$42 \div 6 =$ _____

$6\overline{)24}$

$3\overline{)12}$

9 Karen draws this diagram of a room. What is the area of the room?

1 ☐ = 1 square meter

_____

Identify Number Patterns on the Addition Table

1 (MP) **Reason** Carlos chooses two numbers to add. He follows the rule that the sum must be an even number. What types of numbers can Carlos choose to follow this rule?

_____

Is the sum even or odd? Write *even* or *odd*.

2 $3 + 7$ _____   **3** $2 + 8$ _____   **4** $5 + 6$ _____

Use the Identity Property of Addition to complete the equation.

5 _____ $= 0 + 6$ **6** $9 +$ _____ $= 9$ **7** _____ $+ 0 = 7$

Find the sum. Use the Commutative Property of Addition to write the related addition fact.

8 $4 + 8 =$ _____   **9** _____ $= 3 + 5$ **10** $9 + 2 =$ _____

_____   _____   _____

11 (MP) **Use Structure** Choose a row or a column in the addition table and record the sums. Write the equations below. What patterns do you see in the equations you wrote?

+	0	1	2	3	4	5	6
0							
1							
2							
3							
4							
5							
6							

_____

_____

_____

_____

Test Prep

12 Which is equivalent to 8 + 9?

Ⓐ 8 + 0

Ⓑ 0 + 9

Ⓒ 9 + 8

Ⓓ 80 + 9

13 An equation is shown. Write the unknown number.

$5 + 8 = \boxed{} + 5$

14 Select all that have sums that are odd.

Ⓐ 9 + 2

Ⓑ 3 + 7

Ⓒ 4 + 5

Ⓓ 1 + 6

Ⓔ 8 + 4

15 Use the Identity Property of Addition to complete the equation.

$4 + \boxed{} = 4$

Spiral Review

16 Complete the related facts.

$9 \times \underline{\hspace{1cm}} = 63$

$63 \div 9 = \underline{\hspace{1cm}}$

17 Is the product even or odd? Write *even* or *odd*.

2×7

_____

3×9

_____

© Houghton Mifflin Harcourt Publishing Company

Use Mental Math Strategies for Addition and Subtraction

1 (MP) **Use Tools** At the school picnic, 263 second graders and 198 third graders choose hot dogs to eat. How many hot dogs do the students choose to eat?

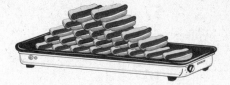

Draw jumps and label the number line to show your thinking.

←———————————————————————→

_____

Use mental math to find the sum or difference.

2 724 − 315 = _____

3 438 + 292 = _____

4 **Math on the Spot** How many students attended school on Tuesday and Wednesday? Explain how you can find your answer.

_____

_____

_____

_____

_____

Harrison School Attendance		
Day	Boys	Girls
Monday	92	104
Tuesday	101	96
Wednesday	105	93
Thursday	99	102
Friday	97	103

Test Prep

5 Add 42 + 105. Which is the sum?

(A) 57

(B) 63

(C) 147

(D) 525

6 Subtract 753 − 198. Which is the difference?

(A) 555

(B) 655

(C) 734

(D) 951

7 What is the sum of 298 and 187?

_____

8 837 − 461 = _____

9 748 + 165 = _____

Spiral Review

10 Multiply or divide.

4 × 3 = _____

8)‾4‾8‾

11 Describe a pattern. Then write a rule and extend your pattern.

12   21   30   39   _____

_____

Name _____

Use Properties to Add

1 (MP) **Use Structure** Ivan plays a video game. He finishes the first 3 levels of the game. How many points does Ivan have after he finishes the first 3 levels of the video game?

Level 1 105 points
Level 2 82 points
Level 3 265 points

_____

Use addition properties to add. Show your work.

2 $44 + 27 + 56 =$ _____

3 $82 + 55 + 38 =$ _____

4 $206 + 114 + 318 =$ _____

5 $125 + 375 + 402 =$ _____

6 **Math on the Spot** Change the order or grouping to find the sum. Explain how you used properties to find the sum.

$59 + 46 + 71$

_____

_____

_____

_____

7 Jane exercises three days this week. She does 76 push-ups on Tuesday, 89 on Thursday, and 54 on Saturday. How many push-ups does Jane do this week?

_____

Test Prep

8 Which is the sum of 32, 98, and 16?

(A) 48

(B) 114

(C) 130

(D) 146

9 Add 243 + 612 + 108. Which is the sum?

(A) 720

(B) 855

(C) 963

(D) 1003

10 What is the sum of 95, 385, and 416?

_____

11 Add 274 + 107 + 336. What is the sum?

_____

Spiral Review

12 Find the unknown number.

$30 \div \boxed{} = 3$

$28 = \boxed{} \times 4$

$\boxed{} \div 6 = 6$

13 One exhibit at the zoo has 4 animal habitats. Each habitat has a 50-gallon water bucket. How many gallons of water do the buckets in the 4 habitats hold?

_____

LESSON 9.4
**More Practice/
Homework**

ONLINE
Video Tutorials and
Interactive Examples

Use Mental Math to Assess Reasonableness

1 (MP) **Critique Reasoning** There are 88 fiction books and 53 nonfiction books in a bookcase. David says there are about 150 books. Is David's statement reasonable? Show your thinking.

_____

2 (MP) **Critique Reasoning** Manuel spends $163 on the electric bill and $98 on groceries. He says he spends about $260. Is his statement reasonable? Explain your thinking.

_____

_____

3 (MP) **Critique Reasoning** A zoo has 158 reptiles in its exhibits. Of those reptiles, 67 are turtles. Tish says there are about 220 reptiles that are not turtles. Is Tish's statement reasonable? Explain your thinking.

_____

_____

_____

4 (MP) **Critique Reasoning** At a store, Beth sees that a camera costs $139 and a printer costs $94. Beth says the cost of the two items is about $150. Is Beth's statement reasonable? Explain your thinking.

_____

_____

Test Prep

5 Mrs. Dominguez buys 288 pencils. She gives 94 pencils to her students. She says that she has about 200 pencils left. Is Mrs. Dominguez's statement reasonable? Explain.

_____

_____

6 Josh saved 173 pennies last month. He saved 103 pennies this month. Josh says he saved about 370 pennies in the two months. Is his statement reasonable? Explain.

_____

_____

7 Mrs. Rozier flies from Atlanta, Georgia to New York City. First, she flies 542 miles from Atlanta to Washington, D.C. Then she changes planes and flies 328 miles from Washington, D.C. to New York City. Mrs. Rozier says she flies about 850 miles. Is her statement reasonable? Explain.

_____

_____

Spiral Review

8 Jake places 24 pictures in 6 equal rows on a wall. How many pictures are in each row?

Write an equation. Use the letter n for the unknown number. Solve.

_____

$n =$ _____

9 Doug reads 30 minutes a day. How many minutes does he read in 7 days?

_____

LESSON 9.5
**More Practice/
Homework**

ONLINE
Video Tutorials and
Interactive Examples

Round to the Nearest Ten or Hundred

1 (MP) **Reason** Lance says that he has about 300 marbles in his collection. Which could the actual number of marbles be? Circle all that could be the actual number of marbles.

30   267   315   242

Explain your answer.

_____

_____

Round to the nearest ten.

2 28 _____   **3** 114 _____   **4** 681 _____

Round to the nearest hundred.

5 265 _____   **6** 650 _____   **7** 129 _____

8 Jamal reads a book with 582 pages. Rounded to the nearest ten, about how many pages does he read?

_____

9 **Math on the Spot** Write five numbers that round to 360 when rounded to the nearest ten.

_____

10 Abdul says the library has about 400 books. What could be the actual number of books? Explain.

_____

_____

Test Prep

11 Round 91 to the nearest ten.

_____

12 Round 91 to the nearest hundred.

_____

13 Round 568 to the nearest hundred.

_____

14 Select all the numbers that round to 400 when rounded to the nearest hundred.

  Ⓐ 418

  Ⓑ 356

  Ⓒ 342

  Ⓓ 439

  Ⓔ 327

15 What is 425 rounded to the nearest 10?

_____

Spiral Review

16 Shay is painting a fence. The fence has 7 sections that are each 4 feet long and one 18-foot-long section. What is the total length of the fence that Shay is painting?

17 Reggie has 8 packages of oatmeal. Each package weighs 10 ounces. How many ounces are in 8 packages of oatmeal?

_____

_____

LESSON 9.6
**More Practice/
Homework**

@Ed **ONLINE**
Video Tutorials and
Interactive Examples

Use Estimation with Sums and Differences

1 **Geography** Austin, the capital of Texas, has an area of 272 square miles. Atlanta, the capital of Georgia, has an area of 134 square miles. The area of Austin, Texas is about how many more square miles greater than the area of Atlanta, Georgia? Explain your thinking.

_____

_____

_____

Estimate the sum or difference. Show your thinking.

2 328 + 280

_____

3 779 + 218

_____

4 541 − 205

_____

5 878 − 106

_____

6 **Math on the Spot** The answer is about 600. What's the question?

_____

_____

Dan's Pet Supplies Sold		
Month	Pet Bowls	Bags of Pet Food
June	91	419
July	57	370
August	76	228

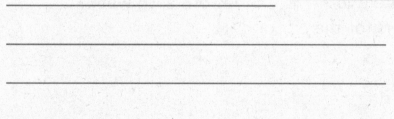

_____

_____

_____

Test Prep

7 Estimate the sum to the nearest ten.

46 + 12

_____

8 Estimate the difference to the nearest hundred.

725 − 361

_____

9 Estimate the difference to the nearest ten.

853 − 509

_____

10 Select all that have sums equal to 600 when each addend is rounded to the nearest hundred.

   Ⓐ 542 + 186

   Ⓑ 218 + 435

   Ⓒ 114 + 392

   Ⓓ 325 + 277

   Ⓔ 481 + 133

Spiral Review

11 Gina earns $9 each day on Tuesday, Thursday, and Friday. Over the weekend, she earns $25. How much money does Gina have now? Write two equations with letters for the unknowns. Solve.

_____

12 Tian takes swim lessons 6 days each week. Each lesson is 50 minutes long. How many minutes does Tian take swim lessons each week?

_____

Use Expanded Form to Add

1 (MP) **Construct Arguments** Priya has 86 blue marbles. She buys the bag of red marbles shown. How many marbles does Priya now have? Explain how you solved the problem.

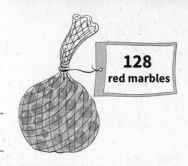

128
red marbles

_____

_____

_____

_____

(MP) **Attend to Precision** Estimate. Then use partial sums to add.

2 Estimate: _____

$269 = $ ☐ $+$ ☐ $+$ ☐
$+\ 32 = $ ☐ $+$ ☐
☐ $=$ ☐ $+$ ☐ $+$ ☐

3 Estimate: _____

$324 = $ ☐ $+$ ☐ $+$ ☐
$+\ 471 = $ ☐ $+$ ☐ $+$ ☐
☐ $=$ ☐ $+$ ☐ $+$ ☐

4 Estimate: _____

$521 = $ ☐ $+$ ☐ $+$ ☐
$+\ 268 = $ ☐ $+$ ☐ $+$ ☐
☐ $=$ ☐ $+$ ☐ $+$ ☐

5 Estimate: _____

$607 = $ ☐ $+$ ☐ $+$ ☐
$+\ 286 = $ ☐ $+$ ☐ $+$ ☐
☐ $=$ ☐ $+$ ☐ $+$ ☐

6 (MP) **Use Structure** A bakery sells 283 banana muffins and 159 blueberry muffins. How many muffins do they sell?

Test Prep

7 Which is the sum of 171 and 84?

    Ⓐ 87

    Ⓑ 155

    Ⓒ 250

    Ⓓ 255

8 Which is the expanded form for 593?

    Ⓐ 5 + 9 + 3

    Ⓑ 50 + 90 + 30

    Ⓒ 500 + 90 + 3

    Ⓓ 500 + 900 + 300

9 Find 496 + 85.

_____

10 Find 427 + 221.

_____

11 What is the sum of 532 and 174?

_____

Spiral Review

12 Is the sum even or odd? Write *even* or *odd*.

    6 + 4 _____

    2 + 5 _____

13 Use regrouping, base-ten blocks, or quick pictures to find the product.

    $40 \times 8 = $ _____

    $20 \times 9 = $ _____

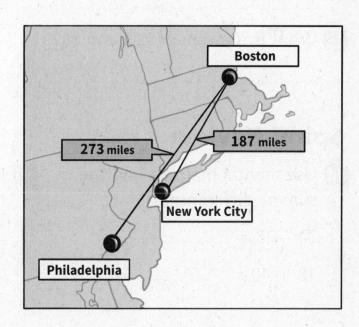
Use Place Value to Add

1 (MP) **Model with Mathematics** On Monday, restaurant workers served 247 lunches and 319 dinners. How many meals did they serve on Monday? Write an equation to model the problem.

_____

(MP) **Attend to Precision** Estimate. Then find the sum.

2 Estimate: _____

```
  208
+  46
```

3 Estimate: _____

```
  579
+  13
```

4 Estimate: _____

```
  623
+ 138
```

5 Estimate: _____

```
  239
+  91
```

6 Estimate: _____

```
  201
+  36
```

7 Estimate: _____

```
  546
+ 429
```

8 **Math on the Spot** A plane flew 187 miles from New York City, New York, to Boston, Massachusetts. It then flew 273 miles from Boston to Philadelphia, Pennsylvania. The plane flew the same distance on the return trip. How many miles did the plane fly?

_____

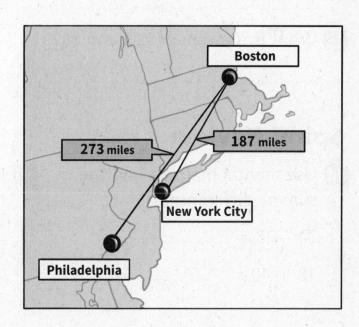

Module 10 • Lesson 2

Test Prep

9 Which is the sum of 779 and 57?

Ⓐ 722
Ⓑ 836
Ⓒ 840
Ⓓ 936

10 Select all that are equal to 512.

Ⓐ 338 + 174
Ⓑ 281 + 231
Ⓒ 502 + 12
Ⓓ 724 + 212
Ⓔ 463 + 49

11 Find 561 + 253.

_____

12 Find 642 + 128.

_____

13 What is the sum of 295 and 86?

_____

Spiral Review

14 Use mental math to find the sum or difference.

34 − 25 = _____

18 + 40 = _____

15 Reggie has 42 crayons that he shares equally with 6 people. How many crayons does each person get?

_____

Combine Place Values to Subtract

1 (MP) **Attend to Precision** Randi works 429 minutes on Tuesday and 256 minutes on Wednesday to build a brick wall. Is the difference between the minutes Randi works on Tuesday and Wednesday greater than 200 minutes? Explain.

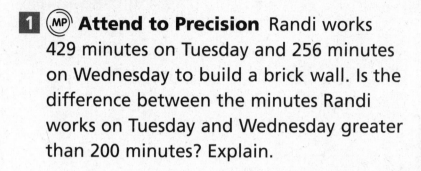

_____

_____

(MP) **Attend to Precision** Estimate. Then combine place values to find the difference.

2 Estimate: _____

$$346 =$$
$$-173 =$$

3 Estimate: _____

$$492 =$$
$$- 64 =$$

4 **Math on the Spot** Alicia sold 47 fewer tickets than Jenna and Matt sold together. How many tickets did Alicia sell? Explain.

_____

_____

_____

| School Play Tickets Sold ||
Student	Number of Tickets
Jenna	304
Matt	159
Sonja	273

5 **Open Ended** Write a word problem for 500 − 137. Solve.

_____

_____

_____

Test Prep

6 Which is the difference?

539 − 162 = ■

- (A) 377
- (B) 467
- (C) 477
- (D) 701

7 Find 913 − 685.

- (A) 48
- (B) 228
- (C) 338
- (D) 388

8 Find 208 − 46.

_____

9 Find 735 − 414.

_____

10 What is the difference?

874 − 529

_____

Spiral Review

11 Use addition properties to add.

64 + 23 + 114 = _____

12 Show another way to group the factors. Find the product.

2 × (3 × 5)

_____

LESSON 10.4
**More Practice/
Homework**

Ed **ONLINE**
Video Tutorials and
Interactive Examples

Use Place Value to Subtract

1 (MP) **Critique Reasoning** Gian and Felicia both solve 781 − 326. Gian says there are not enough ones to subtract 6 ones from 1 one. Felicia says there are enough ones to subtract 6 ones from 1 one. Who is correct? Explain.

_____

_____

(MP) **Attend to Precision** Estimate. Then find the difference.

2 Estimate: _____

$$\begin{array}{r} 83 \\ -35 \\ \hline \end{array}$$

3 Estimate: _____

$$\begin{array}{r} 446 \\ -\ 97 \\ \hline \end{array}$$

4 Estimate: _____

$$\begin{array}{r} 112 \\ -\ 74 \\ \hline \end{array}$$

5 Estimate: _____

$$\begin{array}{r} 631 \\ -148 \\ \hline \end{array}$$

6 **Math on the Spot** What if another roller coaster was 475 feet tall? Which roller coaster would be 230 feet shorter?

Roller Coaster Heights		
Roller Coaster	**State**	**Height in Feet**
Titan	Texas	245
Kingda Ka	New Jersey	456
Intimidator 305	Virginia	305
Top Thrill Dragster	Ohio	420

_____

7 Hugh reads for 112 minutes in a week. Ted reads for 88 minutes. How many minutes longer does Hugh read than Ted?

_____

Test Prep

8 Which is the difference?

$394 - 79 = \blacksquare$

Ⓐ 215   Ⓒ 315

Ⓑ 273   Ⓓ 473

9 Find $282 - 137$.

Ⓐ 145   Ⓒ 319

Ⓑ 155   Ⓓ 419

10 Will the difference for $665 - 572$ be a 2-digit number or a 3-digit number?

_____

11 Find the difference.

$$\begin{array}{r} 780 \\ -\ 647 \\ \hline \end{array}$$

Spiral Review

12 Jake has 64 baseball cards. Marc has 43 baseball cards. Marc says that they have 107 baseball cards. Is his answer reasonable? Explain your thinking.

_____

_____

13 Shana and 3 friends buy a gift for their teacher that costs $36. They each pay the same amount. How much does each person pay?

_____

Name _____

LESSON 10.5
More Practice/ Homework

ONLINE
Video Tutorials and
Interactive Examples

Choose a Strategy to Add or Subtract

1 (MP) **Attend to Precision** A museum has a stamp collection. There are 217 stamps from the United States and 157 stamps from foreign countries on display. Write and solve an equation to find the number of stamps on display. Explain the strategy you used to solve.

_____

_____

_____

Estimate. Then find the sum or difference. Circle the problems in which you need to regroup.

2 Estimate: _____

$$\begin{array}{r} 258 \\ +401 \\ \hline \end{array}$$

3 Estimate: _____

$$\begin{array}{r} 923 \\ -116 \\ \hline \end{array}$$

4 Estimate: _____

$$\begin{array}{r} 672 \\ +249 \\ \hline \end{array}$$

5 (MP) **Reason** Students sell 427 tickets to the county festival. 210 of the tickets are for adults. The rest are for students. Of the tickets sold, are there more adult tickets or student tickets? Explain.

_____

_____

Test Prep

6 A book store display has 82 paperback books and 146 hard cover books. How many books are on the display?

Ⓐ 64   Ⓒ 164

Ⓑ 128   Ⓓ 228

7 Select all that are equal to 207.

Ⓐ 124 + 83

Ⓑ 785 − 627

Ⓒ 192 + 20

Ⓓ 165 + 42

Ⓔ 266 − 59

8 Find 594 − 375.

_____

9 Find 428 + 95.

_____

10 There are 86 members in a choir and 128 members in a concert band. How many more members are in the concert band than in the choir?

_____

Spiral Review

11 Round to the nearest ten.

84 _____

136 _____

12 Each row has 6 seats. There are 3 rows. How many seats are there?

_____

Name _____

Model and Solve Two-Step Problems

1 (MP) **Model with Mathematics** Joanna spends $37 at the mall. She buys the jacket shown and spends the rest of the money on 4 books. How much does each book cost? Write two equations to model the problem. Use letters for the unknown quantities.

$25

_____

_____

2 A sports club has 24 footballs. They have 8 fewer basketballs. How many sports balls does the club have? Write two equations to model the problem. Use letters for the unknown quantities.

_____

_____

3 **Math on the Spot** What if there were 3 students in an election and the total number of votes was 149? What would the bar model for the total number of votes look like? How many votes might each student get?

_____

_____

4 Ed makes 3 bracelets from string. Each bracelet is 10 inches long. Ed starts with 48 inches of string. How many inches of string does Ed have left? Write one equation to model the problem. Use a letter for the unknown quantity.

Test Prep

5 Quinn packs cans of food into 6 boxes. Each box holds 9 cans of food. There are 2 cans that do not fit into the boxes. How many cans does Quinn have?

Ⓐ 17 Ⓒ 54

Ⓑ 52 Ⓓ 56

6 Adam sold 228 carnival tickets on Saturday and 176 carnival tickets on Sunday. His goal is to sell 500 tickets by the end of Monday. How many more tickets does Adam need to sell?

Ⓐ 96 Ⓒ 324

Ⓑ 272 Ⓓ 404

7 Renee puts 8 chairs in each row. She makes 6 rows. She has 3 extra chairs when she is done setting up. How many chairs are there?

_____

Spiral Review

8 Estimate the difference. Show your thinking.

647 − 304 = ▪

_____

_____

_____

9 Count to find the area of the figure.

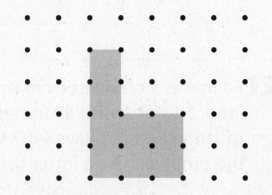

_____ square units

Name _____

LESSON 11.1
More Practice/ Homework

ONLINE
Video Tutorials and
Interactive Examples

Describe Perimeter

1 (MP) **Attend to Precision** Dina draws this figure on dot paper. Describe how to find the perimeter of the figure.

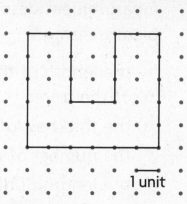

1 unit

_____

_____

Does the situation describe *area* or *perimeter*?

2 The number of square units it takes to cover Quinn's table

_____

3 The number of units it takes to go around Quinn's table

_____

4 **Math on the Spot** Kevin is solving perimeter problems. He counts the units and says the perimeter of the figure is 19 units. Describe the error Kevin made. Circle the places in the drawing of Kevin's solution where he made an error.

Look at Kevin's solution.

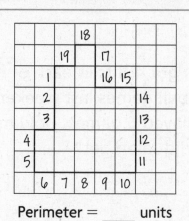

Perimeter = _____ units

Find Kevin's error.

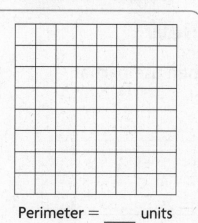

Perimeter = _____ units

_____

_____

Test Prep

5 Shakira is decorating a picture frame. Which measurement describes the perimeter of the picture frame?

(A) the length of the frame multiplied by the width of the frame

(B) the thickness of the wood

(C) the number of pictures that will fit

(D) the length of ribbon edging around the frame

6 Mel's rug has a perimeter of 24 feet. Draw a rectangle that could represent the rug.

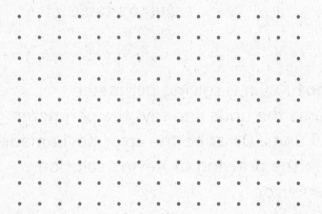

Spiral Review

7 Estimate. Then use partial sums to add.

Estimate: _____

$127 = \boxed{} + \boxed{} + \boxed{}$

$+\ 346 = \boxed{} + \boxed{} + \boxed{}$

$\boxed{} \quad \boxed{} + \boxed{} + \boxed{}$

8 Jalen got 4 hits in each of his baseball games last weekend. He played 6 games. How many hits did Jalen get?

_____

Find Perimeter

1 (MP) **Construct Arguments** Kat and Jim each find the perimeter of the classroom door window. Kat says the perimeter is 30 inches, and Jim says the perimeter is 60 inches. Who is correct? Explain your thinking.

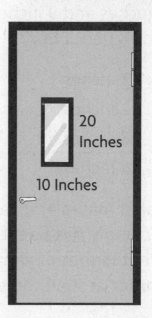

20 Inches

10 Inches

_____

_____

_____

2 (MP) **Attend to Precision** Use a centimeter ruler to measure each side to the nearest centimeter. Find the perimeter.

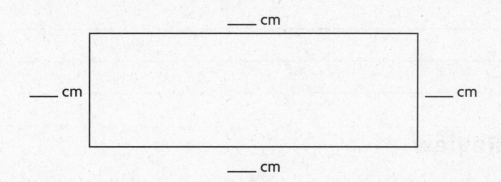

_____ cm

_____ cm

_____ cm

_____ cm

_____

3 **Math on the Spot** Erin is putting a fence around her square garden. Each side of her garden is 5 meters long. The fence costs $4 for each meter. How much will the fence cost?

_____

Test Prep

4 Li's rectangular pencil box has side lengths of 4 inches and 9 inches. What is the perimeter of Li's pencil box?

Ⓐ 13 inches

Ⓑ 22 inches

Ⓒ 26 inches

Ⓓ 36 inches

5 Isabel makes a rectangular drawing on paper. The rectangle has side lengths of 3 inches and 5 inches. What length of yarn does Isabel need to make a border around the edge of her drawing?

_____

6 Tracie has a rectangular rug. Describe how to find the perimeter of the rug.

_____

_____

_____

Spiral Review

7 Estimate. Then find the sum.

384 + 263 = ▪

Estimate: _____

384 + 263 = _____

8 Write a multiplication equation that could be used to solve 12 ÷ 6 = ▪.

_____

Find Unknown Side Lengths

1 (MP) **Use Structure** Vanessa's sheet of paper has a perimeter of 28 inches. What is the unknown side length?

6 inches

s

_____

_____

_____

Find the unknown side lengths.

2 Perimeter = 27 inches

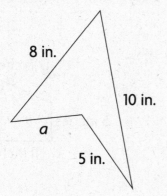

8 in.

10 in.

a

5 in.

a = _____

3 Perimeter = 40 meters

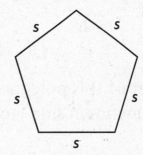

s   s

s   s

s

s = _____

4 (MP) **Reason** A square has a perimeter of 12 feet. Do you have enough information to find the length of each side? Explain.

_____

_____

_____

5 **Math on the Spot** A rectangle has a perimeter of 32 inches. The left side is 7 inches long. What is the length of the top side?

_____

Test Prep

6 The perimeter of a rectangular room is 36 feet. Two of the sides are 8 feet long. What is the length of another side of the room?

Ⓐ 12 feet

Ⓑ 10 feet

Ⓒ 9 feet

Ⓓ 8 feet

7 The perimeter of Dev's square-shaped painting is 20 feet. What is the length of each side of the painting?

_____

8 The perimeter of this polygon is 34 inches. What is the unknown side length?

_____

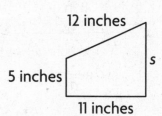

12 inches

5 inches

s

11 inches

Spiral Review

9 Estimate. Then find the difference.

$257 - 62 = $ ■

Estimate: _____

$257 - 62 = $ _____

10 What are the related multiplication and division facts for 8, 9, and 72?

_____

_____

LESSON 11.4
**More Practice/
Homework**

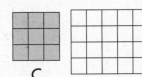
ONLINE
Video Tutorials and
Interactive Examples

Represent Rectangles with the Same Area and Different Perimeters

1 **Math on the Spot** Draw a rectangle with the same perimeter as Rectangle C, but with a smaller area.

C

What is the area?

Area = _____

MP **Use Repeated Reasoning**
Find the area and perimeter. Circle the letter of the rectangle with the *greater* perimeter.

2 *A*

B

3 *C*

D

Rectangle *A*

Area = _____ square units

Perimeter = _____ units

Rectangle *B*

Area = _____ square units

Perimeter = _____ units

Rectangle *C*

Area = _____ square units

Perimeter = _____ units

Rectangle *D*

Area = _____ square units

Perimeter = _____ units

Test Prep

4 Four rectangles have the same area. Which rectangle has the greatest perimeter?

Ⓐ length of 1 foot, width of 12 feet

Ⓑ length of 2 feet, width of 6 feet

Ⓒ length of 3 feet, width of 4 feet

Ⓓ length of 4 feet, width of 3 feet

5 A rectangle has an area of 18 square meters. What is the least perimeter the rectangle can have?

_____

6 Karla wants a fenced garden with an area of 20 square feet. What is the least number of feet of fencing she needs?

_____

7 Ayla wants to make a rectangular picture frame with an area less than 20 square inches. She has 14 inches of ribbon to place around the edge of the picture frame. Draw a rectangle that could represent Ayla's picture frame.

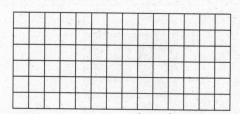

Spiral Review

8 Estimate. Then find the difference.

Estimate: _____

```
  392
- 163
```
☐

9 The drummers are arranged in 8 rows. There are 4 drummers in each row. How many drummers are there?

_____

Name _____

Represent Rectangles with the Same Perimeter and Different Areas

1 (MP) **Attend to Precision** Gina and Stan buy different versions of the class photo. Gina's photo has side lengths of 6 inches and 10 inches. Stan's photo has side lengths of 8 inches and 8 inches. Compare the perimeters and the areas of the photos. Show your work.

	Area	Perimeter
Gina		
Stan		

2 Circle the letter of the rectangle that has a perimeter of 22 units and an area of 24 square units.

A 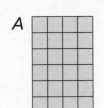   *B*    *C*

3 (MP) **Use Structure** Draw a rectangle that has the same perimeter as the one shown, but with a smaller area.

 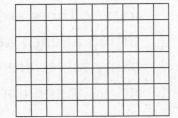

Test Prep

4 Four rectangles have the same perimeter. Which rectangle has the least area?

Ⓐ length of 3 inches, width of 7 inches

Ⓑ length of 2 inches, width of 8 inches

Ⓒ length of 6 inches, width of 4 inches

Ⓓ length of 1 inch, width of 9 inches

5 A rectangle has a perimeter of 16 centimeters. What is the greatest area the rectangle can have?

_____

6 Camille has 32 feet of fencing for a dog run. What is the greatest area she can make the dog run?

_____

7 Draw a rectangle that has the same perimeter as the one shown, but with a greater area.

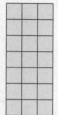 

Spiral Review

8 Jan watches a movie on TV for 180 minutes. During the movie showing, there are 43 minutes of commercials. What is the length of the movie without commercials?

9 There are 56 students in the library. There are 8 students sitting at each table. At how many tables are the students sitting in the library?

Name _____

LESSON 12.1
**More Practice/
Homework**

⊙Ed **ONLINE**
Video Tutorials and
Interactive Examples

Tell and Write Time to the Minute

1 (MP) **Reason** Stephanie looks at the time on a computer. It reads 4:24. Which clock shows the time as 4:24? Explain.

Clock 1   Clock 2

_____

_____

(MP) **Use Tools** Write the time shown on the clock. Then write the time as after the hour or before the hour.

2    **3**

_____   _____

_____   _____

4 **Math on the Spot** What time is it when the hour hand and the minute hand are both pointing to the same number? Aiden says it is 6:30. Camilla says it is 12:00. Who is correct? Explain.

_____

_____

_____

Test Prep

5 Which clock shows the time twelve minutes after seven?

Ⓐ

Ⓒ

Ⓑ

Ⓓ

6 What time does the clock show?

_____

Spiral Review

7 Jen reads 76 pages one week. She reads 115 pages the next week. Jen needs to read 300 pages. How many more pages does Jen need to read? Write two equations that can be used to find how many more pages, *p*, Jen needs to read. Solve.

_____

_____

_____

8 Misha is building a new fence. He has 16 feet of wood. He cuts the wood into 4 equal pieces. What is the length of each piece of wood?

_____

Name _____

Use a.m. and p.m. to Describe Time

1 (MP) **Attend to Precision** Raj starts to cook dinner at the time shown. At what time does he start cooking dinner? Write your answer using a.m. or p.m.

_____

(MP) **Use Tools** Write the time for the activity. Use a.m. or p.m.

2 get ready for bed

_____

3 go grocery shopping

_____

4 **Math on the Spot** From midnight to noon each day, how many times does the minute hand on a clock pass 6? Explain how you found your answer.

_____

_____

_____

5 (MP) **Construct Arguments** Darrell is in Grade 3. He goes to school at 7:25. Is it a.m. or p.m.? Explain your answer.

_____

_____

Test Prep

6 Select all the activities that are done most of the time during a p.m. time.

(A) eat breakfast

(B) use a flashlight outside

(C) get out of school

(D) eat dinner

(E) look at the stars

7 Abdul does his homework when he gets home from school at the time shown on the clock. Write your answer using a.m. or p.m.

Abdul does his homework at _____

Spiral Review

8 Does the situation describe area or perimeter?

The number of units it takes to hang lights around a window

_____

9 Use the Distributive Property to complete the equations. Then find the product.

$7 \times 30 = \blacksquare$

$7 \times 30 = (\underline{\quad} \times \underline{\quad}) + (\underline{\quad} \times \underline{\quad}) + (\underline{\quad} \times \underline{\quad})$

$7 \times 30 = \underline{\quad}$

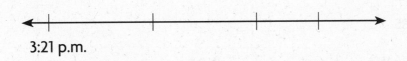

Measure Time Intervals

1 (MP) **Attend to Precision** Wendy begins her homework at 3:21 p.m. and finishes at 3:47 p.m.

Show how to find the elapsed time.

3:21 p.m.

How many minutes does Wendy spend doing her homework?

_____

(MP) **Use Tools** Find the elapsed time.

2 Start at 6:20 p.m.
End at 6:55 p.m.

3 Start at 1:05 a.m.
End at 1:26 a.m.

4 **Math on the Spot** Aiden arrived at the rocket display at 2:25 p.m. and left at 2:58 p.m. Ava arrived at the rocket display at 4:15 p.m. and left at 4:55 p.m. Ava spent how many more minutes at the rocket display than Aiden?

_____

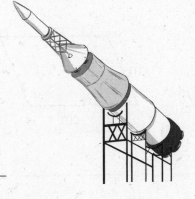

Test Prep

5 Alicia begins walking a dog at 11:02 a.m. and finishes at 11:59 a.m. How long does Alicia walk the dog?

(A) 39 minutes

(B) 47 minutes

(C) 57 minutes

(D) 61 minutes

6 Malik's baseball practice begins at 5:25 p.m. and ends at 5:59 p.m. How long does Malik's baseball practice last?

_____

7 Quinn begins walking to the library at 2:25 p.m. He arrives at the library at 2:48 p.m. How long does it take Quinn to walk to the library?

_____

Spiral Review

8 Use a centimeter ruler to find the length of each side. Find the perimeter.

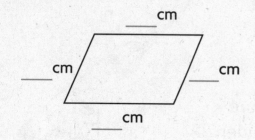

cm

cm

cm

cm

_____

9 Describe a pattern. Then extend the pattern and write a rule.

6   15   24   33   42   _____

Rule: _____.

LESSON 12.4
**More Practice/
Homework**

Ed **ONLINE**
Video Tutorials and
Interactive Examples

Find Start and End Times

1 (MP) **Reason** Sanjay and Karen ride bikes after work. Sanjay starts at 5:15 p.m. and finishes at 5:46 p.m. Karen finishes at 5:54 p.m. She rides for the same amount of time as Sanjay. At what time does Karen start riding? Explain your answer.

_____

_____

2 (MP) **Use Structure** Owen has tasks planned for working on his science project. The number of minutes needed to do each task is shown. Owen starts at 4:00 p.m. Complete the table to show what time he will start and finish each task.

Task	Time Needed	Start Time	End Time
Measure Leaf Lengths	13 minutes	4:00	
Check the Soil	8 minutes		4:24
Plant More Seeds	24 minutes	4:27	

3 **Math on the Spot** Suzi began fishing at 9:45 a.m. and fished until 10:20 a.m. James stopped fishing at 10:50 a.m. He fished for the same length of time as Suzi. At what time did James start fishing? Explain.

_____

_____

Test Prep

4 Cyrus begins cleaning a room at 11:19 a.m. and finishes 35 minutes later. At what time does Cyrus finish cleaning the room?

(A) 10:44 a.m.

(B) 10:49 a.m.

(C) 11:24 a.m.

(D) 11:54 a.m.

5 Veronica practices playing guitar for 28 minutes. She finishes playing at 6:22 p.m. At what time does Veronica begin playing guitar?

_____

6 Diego and Lauren are doing their homework. Diego begins at 4:15 p.m. and finishes at 4:50 p.m. Lauren begins at 5:18 p.m. and spends the same amount of time as Diego. At what time does Lauren finish her homework?

_____

Spiral Review

7 Find the unknown side length.

Perimeter = 49 meters

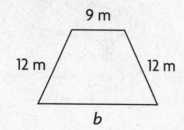

$b =$ _____

8 Use mental math to find the sum or difference.

$56 - 27 =$ _____

$78 + 36 =$ _____

© Houghton Mifflin Harcourt Publishing Company

Solve Time Interval Problems

1 (MP) **Health and Fitness** Josie does 9 minutes of stretches before she runs. She runs for 20 minutes. Then she does 7 minutes of cool down exercises. The clock shows the end time of her workout. At what time does Josie start her workout? Describe how you found the time.

⟷

_____

_____

2 **Critique Reasoning** Jesse writes his Saturday chores on the table shown. Jesse plans to start his chores at 9:05 a.m. He says that if he doesn't take any breaks between tasks, he will be finished with all his chores before 10:00 a.m. Is Jesse correct? Explain your answer.

Chore	Time to complete
Clean bedroom	18 minutes
Mop kitchen floor	15 minutes
Walk the dog	10 minutes

_____

_____

_____

3 **Math on the Spot** When Ethan got home from school, he studied for a test for 35 minutes. Then he spent 15 fewer minutes working on his science project than he did studying for the test. He finished at 4:25 p.m. At what time did Ethan get home from school?

_____

Test Prep

4 Micah will take 15 minutes to get ready for a concert. It will take 18 minutes for Micah to travel to the concert hall. The concert starts at 6:45 p.m. At what time should Micah start getting ready?

Ⓐ 6:12 p.m.   Ⓑ 6:22 p.m.   Ⓒ 6:33 p.m.   Ⓓ 7:18 p.m.

5 Ryan spends 10 minutes drawing. Then he spends 41 minutes on homework. It takes him 12 minutes to clean up before he eats dinner at 5:30 p.m. At what time does Ryan start drawing?

Spiral Review

6 Find the area and perimeter. Circle the letter of the rectangle with the greater perimeter.

A
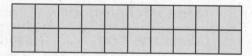

B
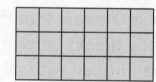

Rectangle *A*

Area = _____ square units

Perimeter = _____ units

Rectangle *B*

Area = _____ square units

Perimeter = _____ units

7 Gia draws this figure. Count to find the area of the figure. Each unit square is 1 square centimeter.

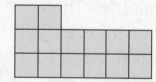

Area = _____ square centimeters

© Houghton Mifflin Harcourt Publishing Company

Name _____

LESSON 13.1
**More Practice/
Homework**

ONLINE
Video Tutorials and
Interactive Examples

Describe Equal Parts of a Whole

1 Zack and Tia have the same sized gardens. Which garden has more room to grow beans? Explain.

Tia's Garden   Zack's Garden

_____

_____

Write whether the shape is divided into *equal* parts or *unequal* parts for 2–4.

2

The parts are

_____.

3

The parts are

_____.

4

The parts are

_____.

5 (MP) **Critique Reasoning** Alex says he divided both of these casserole pans into eighths. Does his statement make sense? Explain.

Casserole Pans

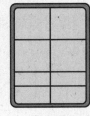

Pan A   Pan B

_____

_____

Write the name for the equal parts for 6–8.

6

_____

7

_____

8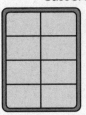

_____

9 **STEM** The steps of the water cycle are precipitation, evaporation, and condensation. Mia divides a poster into thirds to show these steps. Label the rectangle and draw lines to show how Mia could divide her poster.

Test Prep

10 Carmen folds a sheet of paper into halves. Select all the statements that are true.

Ⓐ The paper has equal parts.

Ⓑ The paper is divided into two parts.

Ⓒ Each part of the paper is the same size.

Ⓓ All halves of all sizes of paper are the same size.

Ⓔ A paper folded into thirds has fewer equal parts than Carmen's paper has.

11 Shonda draws a flag. She divides it into fourths. Which could be Shonda's flag?

Ⓐ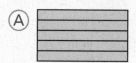

Ⓑ

Ⓒ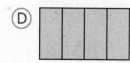

Ⓓ

12 Which shape shows eighths?

Ⓐ   Ⓑ   Ⓒ  Ⓓ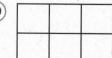

Spiral Review

13 Draw two rectangles that each have a perimeter of 8 units and different areas. Write the areas.

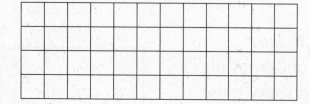

14 Write the products to complete the multiplication table.

×	2	3	4	5	6
2	4	6		10	
4	8	12		20	

LESSON 13.2
**More Practice/
Homework**

ⓔEd **ONLINE**
Video Tutorials and
Interactive Examples

Represent and Name Unit Fractions

1 Soo divides a square into sixths. She colors one of the equal parts red. What fraction of the square is red?

_____

2 ⓂⓅ **Use Structure** The shape shows a unit fraction of a whole. Draw to complete the whole shape. Name the unit fraction.

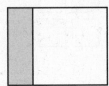 _____

**The shape shows a unit fraction of a group for 3–5.
Draw to complete the group.**

3 a half of a group
$\frac{1}{2}$ ▢

4 an eighth of a group
$\frac{1}{8}$ ◯

5 a third of a group
$\frac{1}{3}$ △

6 ⓂⓅ **Reason** Angela says she drew a square, and the square shows $\frac{1}{2}$ of a whole. Draw to show how the whole could look. Describe how you decided how the whole could look.

_____

_____

Test Prep

7 Which fraction names the shaded part of the whole?

Ⓐ $\frac{1}{2}$

Ⓒ $\frac{1}{4}$

Ⓑ $\frac{1}{3}$

Ⓓ $\frac{1}{8}$

8 Which drawing shows $\frac{1}{3}$ of the group shaded?

Ⓐ

Ⓑ

Ⓒ

Ⓓ

9 A fourth of a shape is shown. Draw to complete the whole shape.

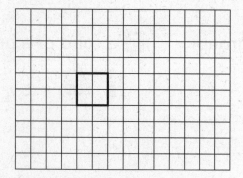

Spiral Review

10 Write the time.

11 Use the Associative Property of Multiplication to find the product.

$3 \times 30 = $ ▪

Represent and Name Fractions of a Whole

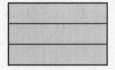 **ONLINE**
Video Tutorials and
Interactive Examples

1 (MP) **Use Repeated Reasoning** Circle the shape that shows $\frac{3}{3}$.

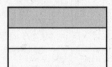 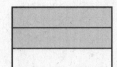 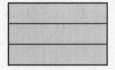

- What pattern can you use to describe how the numerator and denominator change in the fraction models above?

_____

_____

2 Lianne has 4 apples, and $\frac{2}{4}$ of her apples are red. The rest of the apples are green. Draw a picture to show Lianne's apples.

**Write the fraction that names each equal part for 3–4.
Then write a fraction to name the shaded part of the whole.**

3

Each equal part is $\frac{\Box}{\Box}$.

$\frac{\Box}{\Box}$ is shaded.

4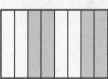

Each equal part is $\frac{\Box}{\Box}$.

$\frac{\Box}{\Box}$ is shaded.

5 **Math on the Spot** Use the picture of the veggie pizza to write a problem that includes a fraction. Solve your problem.

_____

Test Prep

6 Ms. Smith draws a circle on the board. She divides the circle in sixths and shades some of the parts. Select all the circles that could be Mrs. Smith's circle.

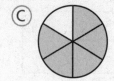

7 Which fraction of the shape does the shaded part represent?

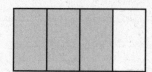

Ⓐ $\frac{2}{4}$

Ⓒ $\frac{3}{4}$

Ⓑ $\frac{2}{6}$

Ⓓ $\frac{3}{6}$

8 Brice shades $\frac{5}{8}$ of a rectangle. How many equal parts are in the whole?

Ⓐ 3

Ⓒ 8

Ⓑ 5

Ⓓ 13

Spiral Review

9 Write the time. Use a.m. or p.m.

20 minutes after 7:00 at night

10 Olive has 48 paintbrushes and 6 boxes. She puts the same number of paintbrushes in each box. How many paintbrushes does she put in each box?

Represent and Name Fractions on a Number Line

1 (MP) **Use Tools** Paul wants to locate $\frac{5}{6}$ on a number line. Complete the number line and draw a point to show $\frac{5}{6}$.

0   1

$\frac{0}{6}$ $\frac{6}{6}$

2 Mr. Walter draws a number line on the board and labels points *A* and *B*. Write the fraction that names each point.

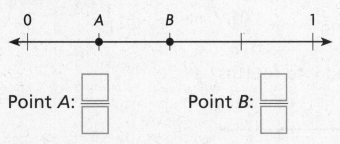

Point *A*: ⬚/⬚   Point *B*: ⬚/⬚

3 (MP) **Reason** Paloma says $\frac{3}{6}$ and $\frac{3}{8}$ are equivalent because both are located 3 marks from 0 on a number line. Is Paloma correct? Explain.

_____

_____

_____

4 **Math on the Spot** Javia ran 8 laps around a track to run a total of 1 mile on Monday. How many laps will she need to run on Tuesday to run $\frac{5}{8}$ of a mile?

_____

_____

_____

Test Prep

5 Which fraction is represented by point *F* on the number line?

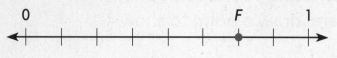

Ⓐ $\frac{6}{8}$ Ⓑ $\frac{8}{6}$ Ⓒ $\frac{4}{6}$ Ⓓ $\frac{1}{8}$

6 Select all the fractions that could name a point that is located on one of the marks on this number line.

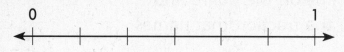

Ⓐ $\frac{5}{8}$ Ⓑ $\frac{6}{8}$ Ⓒ $\frac{3}{6}$ Ⓓ $\frac{7}{6}$ Ⓔ $\frac{1}{6}$

7 Which number line is divided into fourths?

Ⓐ
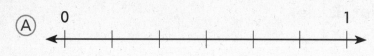

Ⓑ

Ⓒ

Ⓓ

Spiral Review

8 Find the elapsed time.

Start at 5:30 p.m. End at 5:47 p.m.

_____

9 Multiply or divide.

$5 \times \underline{\hspace{1cm}} = 35$

$35 \div 5 = \underline{\hspace{1cm}}$

Name _____

LESSON 13.5
**More Practice/
Homework**

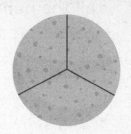
ONLINE
Video Tutorials and
Interactive Examples

Express Whole Numbers as Fractions

1 (MP) **Use Tools** Mason cuts tortillas into thirds. He has 15 thirds. Show how many whole tortillas Mason has. Show your work.

Mason has _____ whole tortillas.

2 Write fractions to complete the number line.

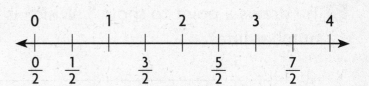

What fraction on the number line is equal to 1? _____

What fraction on the number line is equal to 3? _____

Each shape is 1 whole for 3–4. Write a whole number and a fraction for the parts that are shaded.

3

4

5 **Math on the Spot** Andrea draws the number line. She says that $\frac{9}{8}$ and 1 are equal. Explain her error.

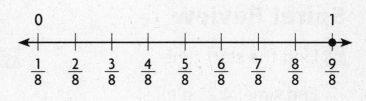

© Houghton Mifflin Harcourt Publishing Company

Test Prep

6 Each circle is 1 whole. Select all the numbers that name the parts that are shaded.

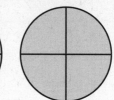

Ⓐ $\frac{20}{5}$

Ⓓ $\frac{20}{4}$

Ⓑ 5

Ⓔ $\frac{5}{4}$

Ⓒ $\frac{25}{5}$

7 Tia draws a point to show $\frac{4}{4}$. Which is Tia's number line?

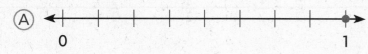

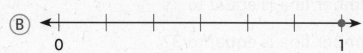

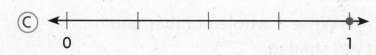

8 Which whole number names the fraction $\frac{12}{3}$?

Ⓐ 4   Ⓑ 3   Ⓒ 12   Ⓓ 6

Spiral Review

9 Find the start time.

End time: 4:27 p.m.

Elapsed time: 15 minutes

10 Find the unknown number.

$4 \times n = 36$

LESSON 13.6
**More Practice/
Homework**

ONLINE
Video Tutorials and
Interactive Examples

Represent and Name Fractions Greater Than 1

1 (MP) **Use Structure** Each shape represents $\frac{1}{3}$ of a whole. How many shapes should be put together to make $\frac{5}{3}$?

$$\boxed{\frac{1}{3}}\ \boxed{\frac{1}{3}}\ \boxed{\frac{1}{3}}$$

_____

2 Taz packs 15 sweaters in boxes. Each box can hold 4 sweaters. How many boxes of sweaters does Taz pack? Write a mixed number for the number of boxes of sweaters Taz packs.

_____

3 Minka pours $\frac{1}{4}$ cup of milk on her oatmeal each day for 7 days. Complete the number line. Draw a point and write the number of cups that Minka pours as a mixed number.

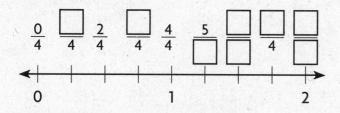

Minka pours _____ cups.

Write the mixed number as a fraction for 4–6.

4 $3\frac{2}{3}$ _____

5 $1\frac{4}{6}$ _____

6 $5\frac{1}{2}$ _____

7 **Open Ended** The shape represents $\frac{1}{2}$ of a whole. To make an amount that is greater than 1, how many shapes will you need? Draw your shapes. Write the mixed number that represents the amount you drew.

$$\boxed{\frac{1}{2}}$$

Test Prep

8 The shape represents 1 whole. Each rectangle represents $\frac{1}{3}$ of a whole. How many rectangles would represent $2\frac{1}{3}$?

$\frac{1}{3}$	$\frac{1}{3}$	$\frac{1}{3}$

   Ⓐ 3   Ⓒ 6

   Ⓑ 4   Ⓓ 7

9 What fraction is represented by the point on the number line?

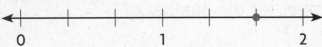

0   1   2

10 Marisol has 5 halves of bread loaves to use to make bread crumbs. How many bread loaves does Marisol have?

   Ⓐ $5\frac{1}{2}$ bread loaves

   Ⓑ 5 bread loaves

   Ⓒ $2\frac{1}{2}$ bread loaves

   Ⓓ $2\frac{1}{4}$ bread loaves

Spiral Review

11 Jay finishes soccer practice at 3:45 p.m. and takes 20 minutes to get dressed. After a 25-minute walk home, Jay starts his homework. At what time does Jay start his homework?

12 Use addition properties to add.

$$17 + 38 + 23 = \underline{\hspace{2cm}}$$

LESSON 13.7
**More Practice/
Homework**

ONLINE
😊 Ed Video Tutorials and
Interactive Examples

Use Fractions to Measure Lengths

1 Measure the length of the line to the nearest half inch. Then measure the length of the same line to the nearest fourth inch. Use a ruler marked with fourth inches.

_____

Nearest half inch: _____

Nearest fourth inch: _____

2 (MP) **Reason** Look at Problem 1. How does using a smaller unit help find a measurement that is closer to the actual length of an object?

_____

_____

_____

Use a ruler marked with fourth inches for 3–5. Measure.

3 What is the length of the pasta to the nearest half inch?

▬▬▬▬

4 What is the length of the ribbon to the nearest fourth inch?

_____   _____

5 **Open Ended** Use a ruler. Measure an object that is less than 5 inches in length to the nearest half inch. Draw your object.

Test Prep

6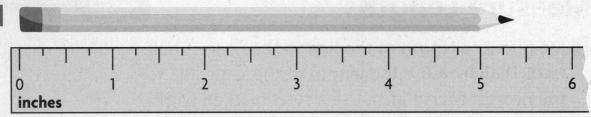

What is the length of the pencil to the nearest half inch?

(A) $4\frac{1}{2}$ inches (B) 5 inches (C) $5\frac{1}{2}$ inches (D) 6 inches

7

Use a ruler marked with fourth inches. What is the length of the crayon to the nearest fourth inch?

_____

8 Use a ruler. Draw a line that has a length of $2\frac{3}{4}$ inches.

Spiral Review

9 Write the name for the equal parts.

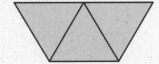

_____

10 Estimate. Then use partial sums to add.

Estimate: _____

$$285 = \boxed{} + \boxed{} + \boxed{}$$
$$+\ 136 = \boxed{} + \boxed{} + \boxed{}$$
$$\boxed{} \quad \boxed{} + \boxed{} + \boxed{}$$

Name _____

LESSON 14.1
**More Practice/
Homework**

ONLINE
Video Tutorials and
Interactive Examples

Relate Fractions and Area

1 (MP) **Attend to Precision** Draw to divide the
square into 4 parts with equal areas.

2 Cross out any shapes that have parts with
unequal areas.

 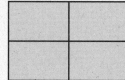 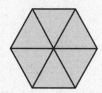

Use the rectangle for 3–4.

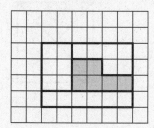

3 Are the 4 parts of the rectangle equal in area? How do
you know?

_____

_____

4 What fraction of the rectangle is shaded gray?

_____

Test Prep

5 Each shape is shaded to represent a fraction. Which shape shows $\frac{1}{3}$ shaded?

Ⓐ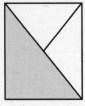

Ⓒ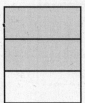

Ⓑ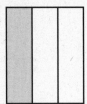

Ⓓ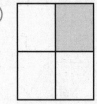

6 What fraction of the triangle is shaded?

_____

7 What fraction of the square is shaded?

_____

Spiral Review

8 Anton has 1 blue stamp and 2 green stamps. What fraction of Anton's stamps is blue?

_____

9 Write the unknown number.

$7 \times 6 = \boxed{} \times 7$

LESSON 14.2
**More Practice/
Homework**

 ONLINE
Video Tutorials and
Interactive Examples

Partition Shapes into Equal Areas

What fraction of the total area of the shape does each equal part represent?

1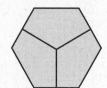

_____   _____   _____

2 (MP) **Critique Reasoning** Dakota says that the drawing on the left shows the only way to divide the square into two equal parts. Lex says there are other ways. Whose reasoning is correct? Use the drawing on the right to help explain your answer.

_____

_____

Use the shapes for 3–4.

3 Shade $\frac{1}{3}$ of the rectangle on the left.

4 Is there another way to divide the rectangle into

3 equal parts? _____

If yes, draw lines on the rectangle on the right to show a way. Shade the rectangle to show $\frac{1}{3}$.

Test Prep

5 Select all shapes in which each part represents the fraction $\frac{1}{4}$.

Ⓐ

Ⓓ

Ⓑ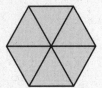

Ⓔ

Ⓒ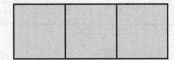

6 Each part of a divided shape represents $\frac{1}{8}$. Into how many equal areas has the shape been divided?

_____

Spiral Review

7 What fraction of the shape is shaded?

_____

8 Find the area of the figure. Show repeated addition. Show multiplication.

Each unit square is 1 meter.

Add. _____

Multiply. _____

Use Unit Fractions to Describe Area

1 What unit fraction of the total area of the circle does each equal part represent?

Each equal part represents _____ of the total area.

2 (MP) **Critique Reasoning** Draw two different ways in which Patti can shade 1 of 6 equal parts of a square. What unit fraction of the square does Patti shade?

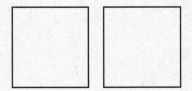

3 Will divides a pizza into 8 equal slices. He sprinkles one slice with extra cheese. On what fraction of the pizza has Will sprinkled extra cheese?

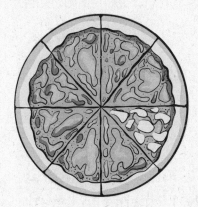

Test Prep

4 Which shape is divided into equal areas that can represent $\frac{1}{3}$?

Ⓐ

Ⓒ

Ⓑ

Ⓓ

5 What unit fraction names each equal part of the shape?

6 Divide the shape into 8 equal areas. What unit fraction names each equal part of the shape?

Spiral Review

7 Draw a point to show $\frac{3}{4}$ on the number line. Label the point.

8 Draw a line that measures exactly $1\frac{1}{4}$ inches in length.

Name _____

LESSON 15.1
More Practice/ Homework

ONLINE
Video Tutorials and
Interactive Examples

Compare Fractions Using Concrete and Visual Models

1 Bianca and Chad are both reading the same book. Bianca has read $\frac{3}{6}$ of the book. Chad has read $\frac{3}{4}$ of the book. Who has read more of the book? Use the visual models to show your work.

Bianca [   ]

Chad [   ]

_____ has read more of the book.

2 **Use Tools** Javier studies for $\frac{1}{2}$ hour on Wednesday and $\frac{1}{3}$ hour on Thursday. Show the fractions on the number lines. Compare the times. On which day does Javier study more?

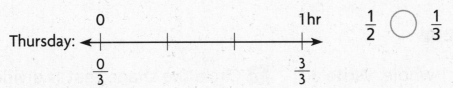

Wednesday: 0   1hr
$\frac{0}{2}$ $\frac{2}{2}$

Thursday: 0   1hr
$\frac{0}{3}$ $\frac{3}{3}$

$\frac{1}{2}$ ◯ $\frac{1}{3}$

Javier studies more on _____.

3 **Math on the Spot** Suri is spreading jam on 8 biscuits for breakfast. She frosted $\frac{1}{2}$ of the biscuits with peach jam, $\frac{1}{4}$ with raspberry jam, $\frac{1}{8}$ with strawberry jam, and $\frac{1}{8}$ with plum jam. Which flavor of jam did Suri use on the most biscuits?

_____

Test Prep

4 Sage and Carla each bake a pie and cut it into 8 equal-sized pieces. Sage serves 4 pieces to her family. Carla serves 1 piece to her family. Who has more pie left?

Complete the drawings to show the number of pieces each pie has left. Write the fractions. Write <, >, or =.

Sage   Carla

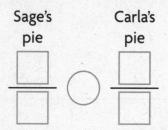

Sage's pie   Carla's pie

_____ has more pie left.

5 Compare the shaded parts of the visual models. Write the fractions. Write <, >, or =.

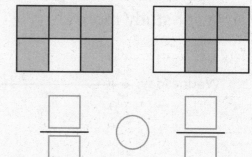

Spiral Review

6 Each shape is 1 whole. Write a fraction and a whole number for the parts that are shaded.

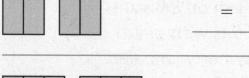

= _____

= _____

7 Circle the shape that is divided into equal areas. What unit fraction names each equal part of the shape?

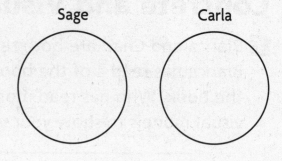

_____

Name _____

Compare Fractions with the Same Denominator

ONLINE
Video Tutorials and Interactive Examples

1 **Math on the Spot** Gary and Vanessa are comparing fractions. Vanessa models $\frac{2}{4}$ and Gary models $\frac{1}{4}$. Vanessa writes $\frac{2}{4} < \frac{1}{4}$. Look at Gary's model and Vanessa's model and describe her error.

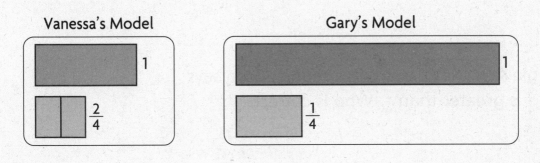

Vanessa's Model

Gary's Model

_____

_____

_____

Compare the fractions. Write <, > or =.

2 $\frac{2}{3}$ ◯ $\frac{1}{3}$

3 $\frac{2}{6}$ ◯ $\frac{5}{6}$

4 $\frac{7}{8}$ ◯ $\frac{5}{8}$

5 $\frac{5}{4}$ ◯ $\frac{5}{4}$

6 Which fraction is less than $\frac{3}{6}$?

(A) $\frac{1}{2}$ (B) $\frac{2}{6}$ (C) $\frac{5}{6}$ (D) $\frac{6}{6}$

Test Prep

7 Which fraction is greater than $\frac{6}{8}$?

Ⓐ $\frac{5}{8}$

Ⓑ $\frac{1}{8}$

Ⓒ $\frac{7}{8}$

Ⓓ $\frac{4}{8}$

8 Maggie says that $\frac{2}{4}$ is greater than $\frac{3}{4}$. Greg says that $\frac{3}{4}$ is greater than $\frac{2}{4}$. Who is correct?

_____

Compare the fractions. Write <, >, or =.

9 $\frac{2}{4}$ ◯ $\frac{3}{4}$

10 $\frac{6}{8}$ ◯ $\frac{3}{8}$

11 $\frac{9}{4}$ ◯ $\frac{5}{4}$

12 Toni walks $\frac{7}{4}$ miles. Ro rides her bike $\frac{5}{4}$ miles. Who travels farther?

_____

Spiral Review

13 Write the fraction as a mixed number.

$\frac{5}{3}$ = _____

$\frac{9}{6}$ = _____

14 Divide the shape into 3 equal areas. What unit fraction names each equal part?

_____

Compare Fractions with the Same Numerator

1 Reason Hector and Zoe each shade same-sized flags. Hector shades $\frac{3}{6}$ of his flag and Zoe shades $\frac{3}{8}$ of her flag. Who shades more? Use the visual models to explain your answer.

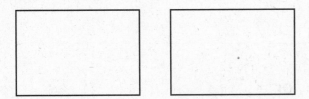

_____

_____

Compare the fractions. Write <, >, or =.

2 $\frac{1}{4}$ ◯ $\frac{1}{3}$ **3** $\frac{5}{6}$ ◯ $\frac{5}{8}$ **4** $\frac{2}{2}$ ◯ $\frac{2}{3}$

5 $\frac{4}{6}$ ◯ $\frac{4}{8}$ **6** $\frac{1}{3}$ ◯ $\frac{1}{3}$ **7** $\frac{3}{8}$ ◯ $\frac{3}{4}$

8 Math on the Spot James ate $\frac{4}{8}$ of his pancake. David ate $\frac{4}{6}$ of his pancake. Who ate more of his pancake? James said he knows he ate more because eight is greater than six. Does his answer make sense?

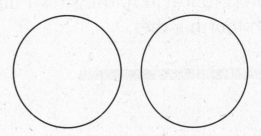

_____

_____

Test Prep

9 Which fraction is greater than $\frac{2}{3}$?

Ⓐ $\frac{2}{4}$

Ⓑ $\frac{2}{8}$

Ⓒ $\frac{2}{6}$

Ⓓ $\frac{2}{2}$

Compare the fractions. Write <, >, or =.

10 $\frac{2}{6}$ ◯ $\frac{2}{8}$

11 $\frac{3}{4}$ ◯ $\frac{3}{3}$

12 $\frac{2}{3}$ ◯ $\frac{2}{3}$

13 $\frac{1}{4}$ ◯ $\frac{1}{6}$

14 $\frac{5}{6}$ ◯ $\frac{5}{6}$

15 $\frac{4}{8}$ ◯ $\frac{4}{4}$

16 Wilson picks $\frac{3}{4}$ pound of berries. Naja picks $\frac{3}{8}$ pound of berries. Who picks less?

_____

Spiral Review

17 Measure the length of the line to the nearest fourth inch. Use a ruler marked with fourth inches.

_____

18 Find the product.

$6 \times 9 = $ _____

Use Reasoning Strategies to Compare Fractions

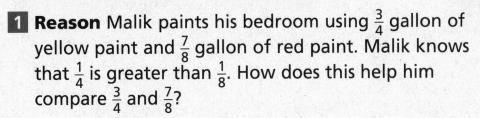

1 **Reason** Malik paints his bedroom using $\frac{3}{4}$ gallon of yellow paint and $\frac{7}{8}$ gallon of red paint. Malik knows that $\frac{1}{4}$ is greater than $\frac{1}{8}$. How does this help him compare $\frac{3}{4}$ and $\frac{7}{8}$?

_____
_____
_____
_____

Compare. Write $<$, $>$, or $=$. Write the strategy you used.

2 $\frac{5}{6} \bigcirc \frac{2}{3}$

3 $\frac{3}{6} \bigcirc \frac{3}{4}$

4 $\frac{1}{4} \bigcirc \frac{3}{4}$

_____   _____   _____

5 **Math on the Spot** Jack says that $\frac{3}{8}$ is greater than $\frac{3}{6}$ because the denominator 8 is greater than the denominator 6. Describe Jack's error. Draw a picture to show your answer.

_____
_____

Test Prep

6 Which fraction is greater than $\frac{5}{6}$?

  Ⓐ $\frac{1}{6}$ Ⓒ $\frac{2}{6}$

  Ⓑ $\frac{5}{8}$ Ⓓ $\frac{7}{8}$

Compare. Write <, >, or =. Write the strategy you used.

7 $\frac{1}{6}$ ◯ $\frac{1}{4}$ _____

8 $\frac{7}{8}$ ◯ $\frac{2}{3}$ _____

9 $\frac{4}{6}$ ◯ $\frac{2}{6}$ _____

10 $\frac{2}{3}$ ◯ $\frac{1}{3}$ _____

11 $\frac{3}{6}$ ◯ $\frac{3}{8}$ _____

12 $\frac{7}{3}$ ◯ $\frac{7}{3}$ _____

Spiral Review

13 Circle the shape that is divided into parts with equal areas.

14 What fraction of the total area of the circle does each equal part of the circle represent?

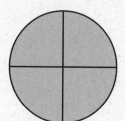

_____

Represent Equivalent Fractions with Smaller Parts

1 (MP) **Critique Reasoning** Bryce says that $\frac{6}{6} < 1$ for the same-sized whole. Is Bryce correct? Explain. Draw to justify your answer.

_____

_____

Locate and draw a point on the number line for the fraction. Then write the equivalent fraction.

2 $\frac{3}{4} = \frac{\boxed{}}{8}$

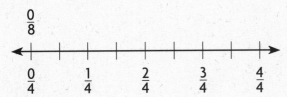

$\frac{0}{8}$

$\frac{0}{4}$ $\frac{1}{4}$ $\frac{2}{4}$ $\frac{3}{4}$ $\frac{4}{4}$

3 $\frac{1}{3} = \frac{\boxed{}}{6}$

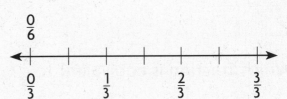

$\frac{0}{6}$

$\frac{0}{3}$ $\frac{1}{3}$ $\frac{2}{3}$ $\frac{3}{3}$

4 **Social Studies** Jed's neighborhood is divided into 2 equal-sized voting areas, the West Side and the East Side. A new voting plan splits the neighborhood into 6 equal-sized areas. Some voters think that the East Side is now smaller in size. Are they right to be concerned? Explain. Make a drawing to help explain your answer.

West Side   East Side

Original Plan

West Side   East Side

New Plan

_____

_____

_____

Test Prep

5 Nia draws two number lines, each divided into equal-sized sections. What point is marked on the first number line?

_____

Draw a point on the second number line to show a fraction equivalent to the fraction on the first number line.

Write the equivalent fractions shown by the points on the two number lines.

6 Which fraction is equivalent to $\frac{1}{3}$?

(A) $\frac{1}{2}$ (B) $\frac{2}{6}$ (C) $\frac{2}{3}$ (D) $\frac{6}{8}$

Spiral Review

7 Divide the shape into 4 equal parts.

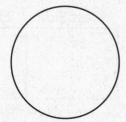

What unit fraction names each equal part of the shape?

8 What fraction of the rectangle does each part represent?

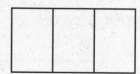

LESSON 16.2
**More Practice/
Homework**

ONLINE
Ed Video Tutorials and
Interactive Examples

Represent Equivalent Fractions with Larger Parts

1 (MP) **Critique Reasoning** Carson and Lydia
have same-sized pizzas. Carson cuts his
pizza into eighths and eats $\frac{3}{8}$. Lydia cuts her
pizza into fourths and eats $\frac{1}{4}$. Carson says
he eats the same amount of pizza as Lydia
because $\frac{3}{8}$ is equivalent to $\frac{1}{4}$. Is Carson correct?
Explain why or why not.

Carson's
Pizza

Lydia's
Pizza

_____

_____

_____

**Locate and draw a point on the number line for the fraction.
Then write the equivalent fraction.**

2 $\frac{8}{8} = \frac{\square}{2}$

3 $\frac{2}{6} = \frac{\square}{3}$

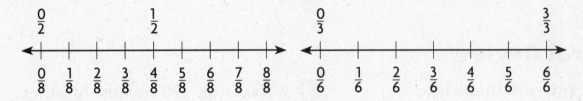

$\frac{0}{2}$ $\frac{1}{2}$

$\frac{0}{8}$ $\frac{1}{8}$ $\frac{2}{8}$ $\frac{3}{8}$ $\frac{4}{8}$ $\frac{5}{8}$ $\frac{6}{8}$ $\frac{7}{8}$ $\frac{8}{8}$

$\frac{0}{3}$ $\frac{3}{3}$

$\frac{0}{6}$ $\frac{1}{6}$ $\frac{2}{6}$ $\frac{3}{6}$ $\frac{4}{6}$ $\frac{5}{6}$ $\frac{6}{6}$

4 (MP) **Use Structure** Keiko bakes two same-sized
pies to sell at a bake sale. She sells $\frac{4}{6}$ of the blueberry
pie. She sells $\frac{2}{3}$ of the apple pie. Are the two fractions
equivalent? Draw a visual model to support your answer.

_____

Test Prep

5 Otis draws lines to divide a circle and shades the parts shown. Divide the same-sized circle another way to show an equivalent fraction.

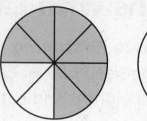 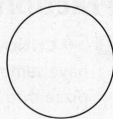

Write the equivalent fractions.

6 Which fraction is equivalent to $\frac{1}{3}$?

Ⓐ $\frac{3}{8}$

Ⓑ $\frac{1}{6}$

Ⓒ $\frac{2}{6}$

Ⓓ $\frac{3}{4}$

Spiral Review

7 Divide the shape into 2 equal parts.

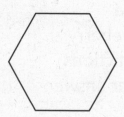

What unit fraction names each equal part of the shape?

_____

8 A town has 129 homes. Another town has 45 homes. Andi says that there are 150 homes in the two towns combined. Is Andi's statement reasonable? Show your thinking.

_____

© Houghton Mifflin Harcourt Publishing Company

LESSON 16.3
**More Practice/
Homework**

ONLINE
Video Tutorials and
Interactive Examples

Recognize and Generate Equivalent Fractions

1 (MP) **Use Structure** Yan and Lila each have same-sized posters. Yan paints $\frac{2}{3}$ of his poster blue. Lila paints the same amount of her poster blue, but she divides her poster into smaller equal-sized sections. What fraction of her poster does Lila paint blue?

Yan's Poster

Lila's Poster

- Shade the posters to show how much each student paints blue.

- Write the fraction that is equivalent to $\frac{2}{3}$. $\dfrac{\square}{\square}$

Circle equal groups to find an equivalent fraction for the shaded area.

2

$$\frac{6}{8} = \frac{\square}{4}$$

3

$$\frac{2}{6} = \frac{\square}{3}$$

4 **Math on the Spot** After dinner, $\frac{1}{3}$ of the cherry pie is left. Suppose 2 friends want to share it equally. What fraction names how much of the whole pie each friend will get? Use the drawing on the right. Explain your answer.

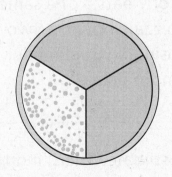

_____

_____

© Houghton Mifflin Harcourt Publishing Company

Test Prep

5 Match the equivalent fractions.

	$\frac{1}{3}$	$\frac{4}{6}$	$\frac{2}{8}$	$\frac{6}{8}$	$\frac{3}{6}$
$\frac{1}{4}$	☐	☐	☐	☐	☐
$\frac{3}{4}$	☐	☐	☐	☐	☐
$\frac{1}{2}$	☐	☐	☐	☐	☐
$\frac{2}{6}$	☐	☐	☐	☐	☐
$\frac{2}{3}$	☐	☐	☐	☐	☐

6 Jensen's dog is supposed to get $\frac{1}{2}$ cup of food every day. All Jensen has is a $\frac{1}{4}$-cup measuring scoop. How many scoops does Jensen need to give her dog

each day? _____

Spiral Review

7 Jordan eats $\frac{3}{6}$ of a small pizza. Tony eats $\frac{3}{8}$ of a same-sized pizza. Show the two fractions using a visual model. Who eats more pizza?

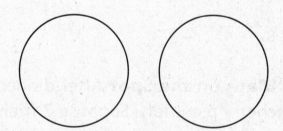

_____

8 Estimate. Then find the sum.

$227 + 519 = \blacksquare$

Estimate: _____

Sum: _____

LESSON 17.1
**More Practice/
Homework**

⊙Ed **ONLINE**
Video Tutorials and
Interactive Examples

Estimate and Measure Liquid Volume

1 Leroy pours water into the container. About how many liters of water are in the container?

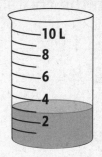

_____

Estimate the liquid volume of the liquid in the container. Write *more than 1 liter, about 1 liter,* or *less than 1 liter*.

2 shampoo bottle

3 pasta pot

4 baby bottle

_____

5 **Math on the Spot** Samuel says that you can pour more liters of water into Container *A* than into Container *C*. Is he correct? Explain.

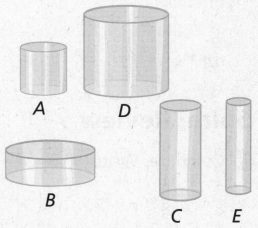

_____

_____

_____

6 **STEM** When water boils, water particles start moving faster and escape into the air. Over time, boiling water loses some of its liquid volume. The liquid volume of water in a pot is 12 liters. After boiling the water for 30 minutes, the liquid volume of the water is now 5 liters less. How many liters of water are left in the pot?

_____

Test Prep

7 About how many liters of water are in the container?

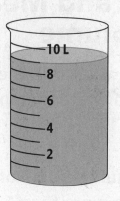

- Ⓐ 1 L
- Ⓑ 8 L
- Ⓒ 9 L
- Ⓓ 10 L

8 Cal and Ernesto have same-sized containers filled with different amounts of water, as shown. Ernesto's container has 15 liters of water. About how much water, in liters, does Cal's container have?

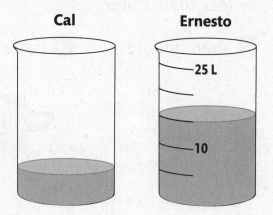

Cal   **Ernesto**

- Ⓐ 25 L
- Ⓑ 15 L
- Ⓒ 5 L
- Ⓓ 1 L

Spiral Review

9 Compare. Write <, >, or =.

 $\frac{3}{8} \bigcirc \frac{5}{8}$

10 Sandra wants to glue a piece of ribbon around the sides of a square-shaped picture frame. The length of each side is 8 inches. What is the length of ribbon that Sandra needs?

Name _____

Estimate and Measure Mass

1 (MP) **Use Tools** The manager at a market is organizing the fruits by mass. He knows that the watermelon has the greatest mass. He wants to put these other fruits in order from least mass to greatest mass.

- Write *greater than* or *less than*.

  The mass of the strawberry is _____

  the mass of the orange.

  The mass of the orange is _____

  the mass of the lemon.

- List the fruits in order from least mass to greatest mass.

  _____

Choose the unit you would use to measure the mass. Write *grams* or *kilograms*.

2 baseball

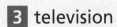

3 television

4 bicycle

_____   _____   _____

5 **Math on the Spot** Amber is buying produce at the grocery store. She says that a Fuji apple and a green bell pepper would have the same mass because they are the same size. Does her statement make sense? Explain.

_____

_____

_____

Test Prep

6 Ivy's sneaker has a mass that is greater than the mass of a pen but less than the mass of a book. Which could be the mass of the sneaker?

- (A) 1 kilogram
- (C) 100 grams
- (B) 3 kilograms
- (D) 3 grams

7 Select all the objects which have a mass that would best be measured using kilograms.

(A)

(C)

(E)

(B)

(D)

8 Cross-Curricular Connection: Financial Literacy
A kilogram of gold has a value of about $39,000. Anthony has a gold pin that is worth $52. Would you measure the mass of Anthony's pin using grams or kilograms? Explain.

_____

_____

Spiral Review

9 Ty runs $\frac{3}{8}$ mile during softball practice and $\frac{5}{8}$ mile during volleyball practice. During which practice does he run farther? How do you know?

_____

_____

10 Draw lines to divide the shape into sixths. Shade $\frac{2}{6}$.

⬜

Name _____

LESSON 17.3
**More Practice/
Homework**

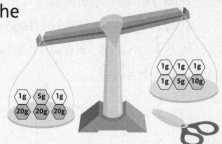

ONLINE
Video Tutorials and
Interactive Examples

Solve Problems About Liquid Volume and Mass

1 (MP) **Reason** If Henri places the scissors on the right pan, the two pans will be balanced. What is the mass of the scissors?

• Show your work.

• The mass of the scissors is _____.

2 The table shows about how many liters of water people use in different countries. What is the difference between the least amount and greatest amount of water used?

Country	Water Used by One Person in One Day
Canada	329 L
Mexico	165 L
U.S.	340 L

3 **Math on the Spot** Ellen will pour water into Pitcher B until it has 1 more liter of water than Pitcher A. How many liters of water will she pour into Pitcher B? Explain how you found your answer.

Pitcher A

Pitcher B

© Houghton Mifflin Harcourt Publishing Company

Test Prep

4 Paco has some toy cars that are all the same. Each toy car has the mass shown. The total mass of the toy cars is 63 grams. How many toy cars does Paco have?

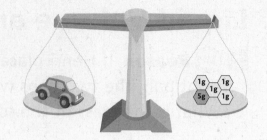

- (A) 7
- (B) 9
- (C) 54
- (D) 72

5 Katerina and Erik have same-sized containers with different amounts of water. About how many more liters of water does Erik have than Katerina?

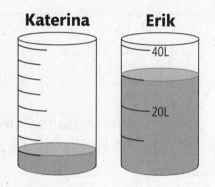

- (A) 25 liters
- (B) 30 liters
- (C) 35 liters
- (D) 40 liters

Spiral Review

6 Compare. Write <, >, or =.

$\frac{6}{8} \bigcirc \frac{6}{9}$

7 Measure the length of the key to the nearest fourth inch.

LESSON 18.1
**More Practice/
Homework**

ONLINE
Video Tutorials and
Interactive Examples

Use Picture Graphs

Use the graph for 1–4.

Carmen makes a picture graph of players' scores for a game.

1 How many more points does Carmen score than Indira?

_____

2 How many fewer points does Nyeema score than Benji?

_____

3 Players who score greater than 50 points get a free game. Which players score greater than 50 points?

_____

Game Scores	
Carmen	★ ★ ★ ★ ★ ★ ★ ★
Benji	★ ★ ★ ★ ★⌐
Deb	★ ★ ★⌐
Indira	★ ★ ★ ★ ★
Nyeema	★ ★

Key: Each ★ = 10 points.

4 (MP) **Model with Mathematics** Kyrie scores 25 fewer points than Carmen. How many points does Kyrie score? Write an equation you can use to solve the problem. Explain.

_____

_____

5 **Math on the Spot** The students who went to summer camp voted for their favorite activity. Which two activities received a total of 39 votes?

Favorite Camp Activity	
Biking	☺ ☺ ☺ ☾
Hiking	☺ ☺ ☺ ☺
Boating	☺ ☺ ☺
Fishing	☺ ☾

Key: Each ☺ = 6 students.

_____

Test Prep

6 Hanna's picture graph shows how many people attend a club or activity on different days. How many more people attend a club or activity on Saturday than on Friday?

Ⓐ 8   Ⓒ 2

Ⓑ 4   Ⓓ 1

Club or Activity Attendance	
Wednesday	☺ ☺ ☺ ☺
Thursday	☺ ☺ ☺ ☺ ☺ ☺
Friday	☺ ☺ ☺ ◖
Saturday	☺ ☺ ☺ ☺ ☺ ◖
Sunday	☺ ☺ ☺
Key: Each ☺ = 4 people.	

7 Amelia surveys her classmates about their favorite types of games. Her data is shown in the table. Complete the picture graph.

Favorite Game	
Puzzles	6
Board Games	10
Card Games	8

Favorite Game	
Puzzles	✔ ✔ ✔
Board Games	✔ ✔ ✔ ✔ ✔
Card Games	
Key: Each ✔ = 2 students.	

Spiral Review

8 Ada shades $\frac{1}{2}$ of a circle. Show an equivalent fraction on the same-sized circle. Write the equivalent fraction.

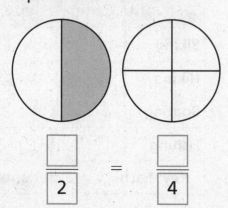

$$\frac{\Box}{2} = \frac{\Box}{4}$$

9 Divide the shape so that each part is $\frac{1}{8}$ of the whole shape's area.

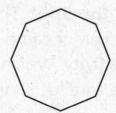

LESSON 18.2
**More Practice/
Homework**

📧 **Ed** **ONLINE**
Video Tutorials and
Interactive Examples

Make Picture Graphs

Use the data in the table for 1–4.

A store manager records in a table
the number of computer tablets sold
during a weekend.

Computer Tablet Sales	
Day	Tablets
Friday	35
Saturday	50
Sunday	40
Monday	25

1 (MP) **Attend to Precision** Make a picture graph
that shows the data. Choose a number greater
than 1 for what the symbol represents.

2 (MP) **Reason** Explain how you chose
the key.

_____

_____

_____

_____

Friday	
Saturday	
Sunday	
Monday	

Key: Each _____ = _____ tablets.

3 How many more computer tablets
are sold on Sunday than Monday?

_____

4 How many fewer computer tablets are sold on Friday
than Sunday?

_____

5 **Open Ended** How is making a picture graph like
representing equal groups?

_____

_____

Test Prep

Use the data in the table for 6–7.

6 Phil surveys his friends about their favorite kind of music. His data is shown in the table. Make a picture graph that represents the data.

Favorite Music	
Kind of Music	**Number of Friends**
Classical	3
Rock	6
Pop	8
Hip-Hop	7

Favorite Music	
Classical	
Rock	
Pop	
Hip-Hop	

Key: Each   = 2 friends.

7 How many more friends choose pop music than classical music?

- Ⓐ 3
- Ⓑ 4
- Ⓒ 5
- Ⓓ 8

Spiral Review

8 Each shape is 1 whole. Shade the shape to show the equivalent fraction. Write the equivalent fraction.

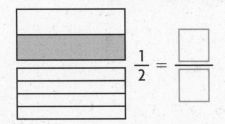

$\frac{1}{2} = \frac{\square}{\square}$

9 Find the product.

$4 \times 60 = $ _____

© Houghton Mifflin Harcourt Publishing Company

LESSON 18.3
More Practice/ Homework

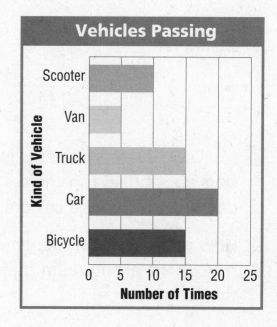
ONLINE
Video Tutorials and
Interactive Examples

Use Bar Graphs

Use the bar graph for 1–6.

Mitch watches vehicles pass the library. He records in a bar graph the number of times he sees each type of vehicle.

1 Which type of vehicle passes the library the greatest number of times?

_____

2 Which type of vehicle passes the library the least number of times?

_____

3 How many more times does a car pass than a van?

_____

4 How many fewer times does a scooter pass than a bicycle?

_____

5 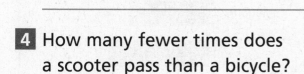 **Critique Reasoning** Norma says that if the graph is changed to a vertical bar graph, the numbers for the data would be greater. Is Norma correct? Explain.

_____

_____

_____

6 **Open Ended** Write a word problem using the information in the bar graph.

_____

Test Prep

7 Kayla surveys her friends about their favorite sneaker color. Her data is shown in the bar graph.

How many more friends choose purple sneakers than pink sneakers?

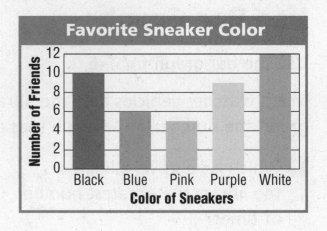

Favorite Sneaker Color

(A) 4   (C) 9

(B) 5   (D) 14

8 Ms. Davis surveys students in the class about field trip choices. Her data is shown in the bar graph.

How many fewer students choose the art museum than the farm?

_____

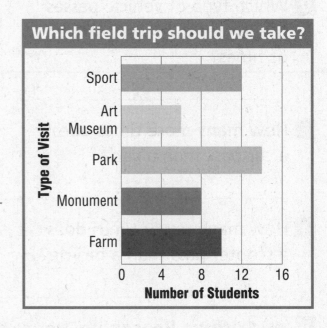

Which field trip should we take?

Spiral Review

9 Estimate the liquid volume when each container is filled. Write *more than 1 liter, about 1 liter,* or *less than 1 liter.*

Glass of water

_____

Large fish tank

_____

10 Divide the shape into 4 parts with equal areas. Write the unit fraction that names each equal part of the shape.

_____

LESSON 18.4
**More Practice/
Homework**

ONLINE
Video Tutorials and
Interactive Examples

Make Bar Graphs

Use the data in the table for 1–6.

Lupe records data about the number of miles she runs each week. Her data is shown in the table.

Miles Run Each Week	
Week	**Number of Miles**
1	20
2	5
3	10
4	15
5	5

1 (MP) **Attend to Precision** Make a horizontal bar graph that shows the data in the table.

2 Choose a scale that is greater than 1. What number will you count by on the scale?

_____

3 How many fewer miles does Lupe run in Week 4 than in Week 1?

_____

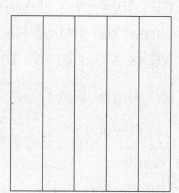

4 How many more miles does Lupe run in Week 1 than in Week 5?

_____

5 (MP) **Critique Reasoning** Nash says that if Lupe runs 5 more miles in Week 5, the bar would be drawn longer to show 15. Is Nash correct? Explain.

_____

_____

6 **Open Ended** Write and solve a word problem using the information in your bar graph.

_____

_____

Test Prep

7 Lexi surveys her classmates about their favorite sport to play. Her data is shown in the table. Complete the bar graph.

Favorite Sport	
Kind of Sport	Number of Classmates
Baseball	2
Basketball	10
Soccer	4
Volleyball	6

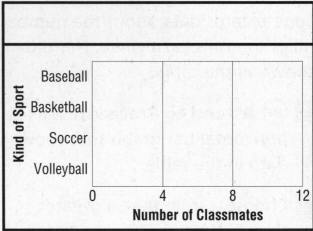

8 Gil surveys his classmates about their favorite cereal bar flavor. His data is shown in the table. Make a bar graph that represents the data.

Favorite Flavor of Cereal Bar	
Flavor	Number of Students
Apple	8
Blueberry	3
Lemon	5
Oatmeal	7
Raisin	10

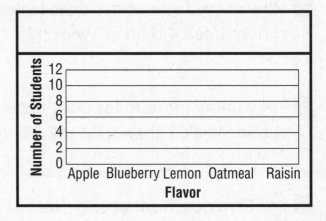

Spiral Review

9 Chris uses less than 1 liter of water to fill a container. Is he most likely filling a bowl, a jug, or a bathtub?

10 Draw lines to divide the shape into 3 parts with equal areas. What unit fraction names each equal part of the shape?

Name _____

LESSON 18.5
More Practice/ Homework

 ONLINE
Video Tutorials and
Interactive Examples

Use Line Plots to Display Measurement Data

(MP) **Use Structure** Use the line plot for 1–5.

Tori collects candlesticks. She measures the height of each candlestick in her collection.

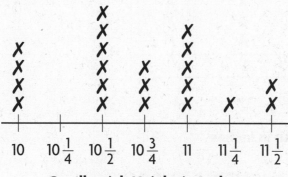

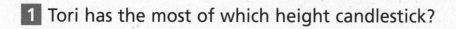

$$10 \quad 10\frac{1}{4} \quad 10\frac{1}{2} \quad 10\frac{3}{4} \quad 11 \quad 11\frac{1}{4} \quad 11\frac{1}{2}$$

Candlestick Height in Inches

1 Tori has the most of which height candlestick?

_____

2 Tori has no candlesticks with a height

of _____ inches.

3 What is the height of Tori's shortest candlestick?

_____

4 How many of Tori's candlesticks have heights of 11 inches or longer?

_____

5 How many more candlesticks have a height of $10\frac{3}{4}$ inches than a height of $11\frac{1}{2}$ inches?

_____

Test Prep

Use the line plot for 6–7.

Nora makes bowls out of clay. The bowls have different widths.

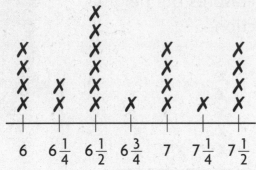

Bowl Width in Inches

6 How many bowls does Nora make that have a width of less than 7 inches?

(A) 4 bowls   (C) 13 bowls

(B) 9 bowls   (D) 17 bowls

7 Nora makes how many more bowls with a width of $6\frac{1}{2}$ inches than $7\frac{1}{2}$ inches? Show your work.

Spiral Review

8 Choose the unit you would use to measure the mass. Write *gram* or *kilogram*.

a grape _____

a bag of potatoes _____

9 Draw lines to divide the shape into 2 parts with equal areas.

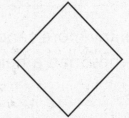

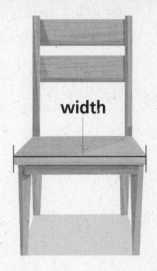
Make Line Plots to Display Measurement Data

1 (MP) **Attend to Precision** Measure and record the width of some chair seats to the nearest half inch.

• Make a line plot to show the data.

width

┼──┼──┼──┼──┼──┼──┼──┼──┼──┼──┼──┼──┼──┼──

(MP) **Use Structure** Use your line plot for 2–4.

2 Which chair seat width appears most often?

_____

3 Which chair seat width appears least often?

_____

4 Is there any width for which there is no data? Explain.

_____

_____

5 **Math on the Spot** Garden club members recorded the height of their avocado plants to the nearest inch in a line plot. How many more plants are 8 or 9 inches tall than 6 or 7 inches tall? Explain.

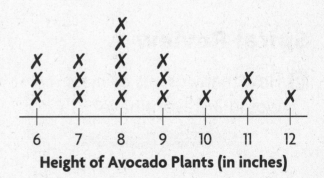

Height of Avocado Plants (in inches)

_____

_____

Test Prep

6 Janda measures the length of 10 used erasers to the nearest quarter inch. Her data is shown in the table. Complete the line plot.

Eraser Length in Inches	Tally
$2\frac{1}{4}$	I
2	IIII
$1\frac{3}{4}$	III
$1\frac{1}{4}$	I

Eraser Lengths in Inches

7 Dean measures the lengths of 12 pieces of used chalk to the nearest half inch. Make a line plot to show the data.

$2\frac{1}{2}$, $1\frac{1}{2}$, 2, $1\frac{1}{2}$,

2, 1, $1\frac{1}{2}$, $1\frac{1}{2}$,

2, $\frac{1}{2}$, $1\frac{1}{2}$, $2\frac{1}{2}$

Spiral Review

8 How many grams of mass would 3 crayons have?

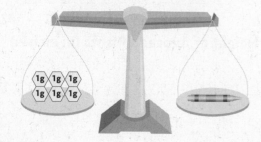

9 Draw lines to divide the shape into 6 parts with equal areas. What fraction names one of the equal parts?

LESSON 18.7
More Practice/Homework

Solve One- and Two-Step Problems Using Data

ONLINE
Video Tutorials and
Interactive Examples

(MP) **Attend to Precision** Use the data in the table for 1–3.

Nut Lengths in Inches		
$\frac{1}{2}$ inch	$\frac{3}{4}$ inch	1 inch
$\frac{3}{4}$ inch	1 inch	$\frac{3}{4}$ inch
1 inch	$\frac{1}{4}$ inch	1 inch

Kirk measures the lengths of some almond nuts to the nearest quarter inch. How many fewer nuts have lengths of $\frac{1}{4}$ inch and $\frac{1}{2}$ inch combined than a length of 1 inch?

1 Make a line plot to show the data.

2 How many fewer nuts have lengths of $\frac{1}{4}$ inch and $\frac{1}{2}$ inch combined than a length of 1 inch?

_____

3 How would you compare the number of different-length nuts using a picture graph?

_____

4 **Math on the Spot** How many DVDs does Diego have that are NOT comedy DVDs?

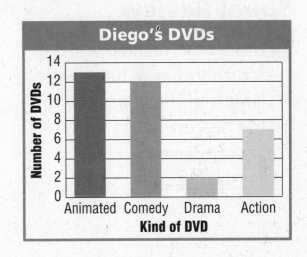

Test Prep

Use the data in the table for 5–6.

5 Wendi surveys her classmates about their favorite hobbies. Her data is shown in the table. Complete the bar graph that represents the data.

Favorite Hobbies	
Hobby	Number of Students
Art	2
Music	8
Photography	7
Sports	9
Writing	4

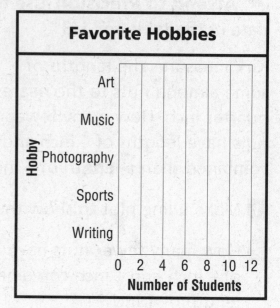

6 How many more students choose sports than art and writing combined?

Ⓐ 2　　　　Ⓑ 3　　　　Ⓒ 9　　　　Ⓓ 15

Spiral Review

7 Use a ruler marked with fourth inches. What is the length of the paper clip to the nearest fourth inch?

8 Do the parts of the rectangle have the same area? How do you know? What fraction of the total area of the rectangle is the shaded part?

© Houghton Mifflin Harcourt Publishing Company

Name _____

LESSON 19.1
More Practice/ Homework

ONLINE
Ed
Video Tutorials and
Interactive Examples

Describe Shapes

1 (MP) **Critique Reasoning** Abby says that a plane shape and a polygon are the same. Is she correct? Explain.

_____

_____

_____

Is the shape a polygon? Write *yes* or *no.*

2

_____

3

_____

4

_____

Write the number of sides and the number of angles.

5

_____ sides

_____ angles

6
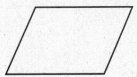

_____ sides

_____ angles

7

_____ sides

_____ angles

8 **Math on the Spot** Draw a closed shape by connecting 5 line segments at their endpoints.

Test Prep

9 Which is a plane shape but not a polygon?

 Ⓐ   Ⓑ   Ⓒ   Ⓓ

10 How many sides does this polygon have?

Ⓐ 6   Ⓒ 10

Ⓑ 8   Ⓓ 12

11 Circle the open shape. Put an *X* on the closed shape.

   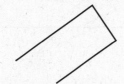

Spiral Review

12 Students voted for their favorite fruit. The results are in the table below. Make a picture graph to show the data. Choose a scale that is greater than 1.

Favorite Fruit	
Fruit	**Votes**
Bananas	6
Apples	10
Pears	2
Peaches	4
Grapes	7

Key: Each _____ = _____ votes.

LESSON 19.2
**More Practice/
Homework**

⊙Ed **ONLINE**
Video Tutorials and
Interactive Examples

Describe Angles in Shapes

1 (MP) **Use Tools** Sean wants to compare one
angle of a shape to a right angle. Explain
how Sean can use a tool to compare the angle.

_____

_____

_____

**Write the total number of each kind of angle. Draw a
small square to mark what appears to be a right angle.**

2
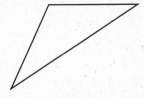

_____ right

_____ less than right

_____ greater than right

3

_____ right

_____ less than right

_____ greater than right

4 **Math on the Spot** Describe the types of angles
formed when you divide a circle into 4 equal parts.

_____

5 **Open Ended** Name an object that has a right angle.
Draw your object. Mark what appears to be a right angle.

_____

6 **Health and Fitness** In PE, Eva learns about
ballet and the fifth position of her feet. She
says that her feet have formed an angle. Has
Eva formed a right angle, greater than a right
angle, or less than a right angle with her feet?

_____

© Houghton Mifflin Harcourt Publishing Company

Test Prep

7 How many angles in this shape appear to be greater than a right angle?

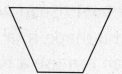

(A) 4

(C) 1

(B) 2

(D) 0

8 Select all the shapes that appear to have at least one right angle.

(A)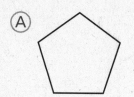

(D)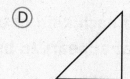

(B)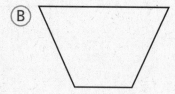

(E)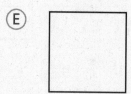

(C)

Spiral Review

Use the graph for 9–10.

9 How many fewer students choose cats than dogs as their favorite pet?

_____

10 How many more students choose dogs than fish and reptiles combined?

_____

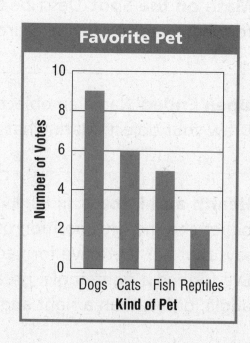

Name _____

LESSON 19.3
More Practice/Homework

 ONLINE
Video Tutorials and
Interactive Examples

Describe Sides of Shapes

1 (MP) **Critique Reasoning** Dre says a closed shape cannot have exactly 3 sides and one pair of parallel sides. Is Dre correct? Explain.

_____

_____

Write _equal length_ or _not equal length_ to describe the gray sides of the shape.

2    **3** 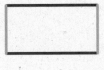   **4**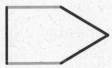

_____   _____   _____

Look at the gray sides of the shape. Write if they appear to be _parallel_ or _not parallel_.

5   **6**   **7**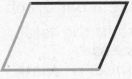

_____   _____   _____

8 (MP) **Construct Arguments** This shape is drawn on the board. Grace says the shape's gray sides appear to be parallel. Oscar says the shape's gray sides do not appear to be parallel. Who is correct? Explain.

_____

_____

Test Prep

9 Which shape has exactly 1 pair of sides that appears to be the same distance apart?

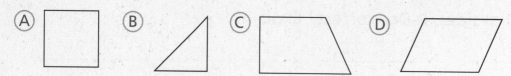

Ⓐ   Ⓑ   Ⓒ   Ⓓ

10 Which shape has gray sides that appear to be of equal length?

Ⓐ   Ⓒ

Ⓑ   Ⓓ

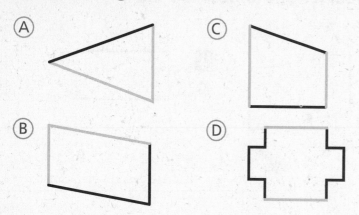

Spiral Review

11 Make a bar graph that shows the data in the table.

Number of Math Problems Solved

Days	Tally
Monday	𝍤 𝍤 𝍤
Tuesday	𝍤 |||
Wednesday	𝍤 𝍤
Thursday	𝍤
Friday	𝍤 𝍤 ||

LESSON 19.4
**More Practice/
Homework**

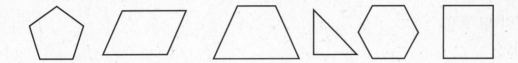

ONLINE
Video Tutorials and
Interactive Examples

Define Quadrilaterals

1 Circle the shapes that are quadrilaterals.

Circle all the words that describe the quadrilateral.

Define a trapezoid as a quadrilateral that has *exactly* 1 pair of parallel sides.

2 	3	4 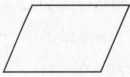
parallelogram	parallelogram	parallelogram
quadrilateral	quadrilateral	quadrilateral
rectangle	rectangle	rectangle
rhombus	rhombus	rhombus
square	square	square
trapezoid	trapezoid	trapezoid

(MP) **Reason** Write *all* or *some* to complete the sentences.

5 _____ sides of a
parallelogram are equal
in length.

6 _____ rectangles
are squares.

7 **Math on the Spot** I am a polygon that has 4 sides and
4 angles. At least one of my angles is less than a right
angle. Circle all the shapes that I could be.

    quadrilateral   rectangle   square   rhombus   trapezoid

Test Prep

8 Which shape always has 4 sides that are equal in length and can have no right angles?

Ⓐ parallelogram

Ⓑ rhombus

Ⓒ square

Ⓓ rectangle

9 Select all the shapes that are quadrilaterals.

Ⓐ triangle

Ⓑ trapezoid

Ⓒ rhombus

Ⓓ pentagon

Ⓔ square

10 Write *all* or *some* to complete the sentence.

_____ squares are rhombuses.

11 Write *all* or *some* to complete the sentence.

_____ parallelograms are rectangles.

Spiral Review

12 Tristan measures each of the carrots that he buys at the grocery store. He uses a line plot to record the length of each carrot.

How many carrots have a length greater than 6 inches?

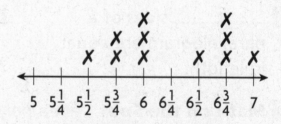

Carrot Lengths in Inches

_____

© Houghton Mifflin Harcourt Publishing Company

Name _____

Draw Quadrilaterals

1 (MP) **Reason** Draw a quadrilateral that does not belong to the group. Then explain why it does not belong.

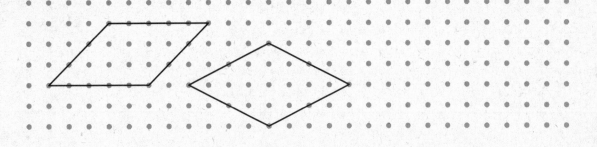

_____

_____

Draw and name the quadrilateral.

2 4 sides of equal length, 4 right angles

3 2 pairs of sides of equal length, no right angles

_____ _____

4 **Math on the Spot** Amy has 4 straws of equal length. Name all the quadrilaterals that she can make using these straws.

_____

Amy cuts one of the straws in half. She uses the two halves and two of the other straws to make a quadrilateral. Name all the quadrilaterals that can be made using these 4 straws.

_____

Test Prep

5 Draw a quadrilateral with 4 right angles and 2 pairs of opposite sides that are equal in length.

6 Which is the name of a shape that is a quadrilateral but not a rhombus?

Ⓐ square

Ⓒ rectangle

Ⓑ triangle

Ⓓ hexagon

7 Which shape has 4 sides of equal length and may have no right angles?

Ⓐ square

Ⓒ triangle

Ⓑ rhombus

Ⓓ rectangle

Spiral Review

8 Use a ruler marked with quarter inches. Measure and record the length of each line to the nearest quarter inch.

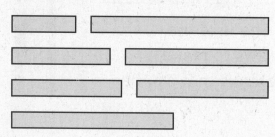

9 Make a line plot that shows the data from Problem 8.

© Houghton Mifflin Harcourt Publishing Company

Name

LESSON 20.2
**More Practice/
Homework**

ONLINE
Video Tutorials and
Interactive Examples

Categorize Quadrilaterals

1 (MP) Construct Arguments

- Is a parallelogram always a rhombus? Explain.

_____

_____

_____

- Is a rhombus always a parallelogram? Explain.

_____

_____

_____

2 Circle the shapes that are trapezoids when a trapezoid
is defined as a quadrilateral that has *exactly* one pair of
parallel sides.

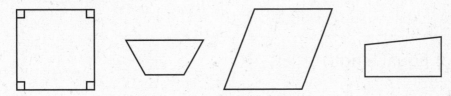

3 (MP) **Construct Arguments** Explain why a square is always
a rhombus.

_____

_____

4 (MP) **Attend to Precision** Circle the words that describe
the shape shown. Define a trapezoid as a quadrilateral
that has *at least* 1 pair of parallel sides.

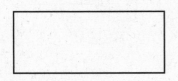

parallelogram   rhombus

quadrilateral   square

rectangle   trapezoid

Test Prep

5 Select all the quadrilaterals that *always* have 4 right angles.

  (A) parallelogram   (D) rhombus

  (B) rectangle   (E) trapezoid

  (C) square

6 Which word describes the shape shown?

  (A) parallelogram   (C) trapezoid

  (B) rhombus   (D) quadrilateral

7 Which polygon *always* has all of the following?

- 4 right angles

- all sides are of equal length

- quadrilateral

  (A) square   (C) parallelogram

  (B) rhombus   (D) rectangle

Spiral Review

8 Draw a line that is exactly $2\frac{1}{4}$ inches in length.

9 Circle the shape that is divided into parts with equal areas.

LESSON 20.3
**More Practice/
Homework**

ⓔEd **ONLINE**
Video Tutorials and
Interactive Examples

Categorize Plane Shapes

Complete the Venn diagram.

1 Place the letter of each
shape in the correct place
in the Venn diagram.

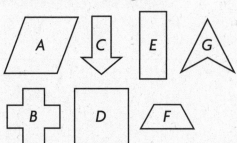

Quadrilaterals   Polygons
with at least
2 right angles

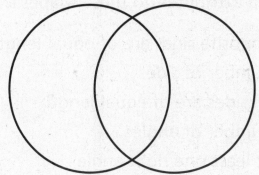

2 ⓜⓟ **Construct Arguments** Is a triangle a polygon, a
quadrilateral, or both? Explain.

_____

_____

3 **Math on the Spot** Label the Venn diagram to show
one way you can sort a parallelogram, a rectangle, a
square, a trapezoid, and a rhombus.

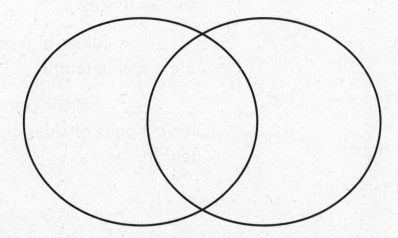

© Houghton Mifflin Harcourt Publishing Company

Test Prep

4 A rectangle and a trapezoid are shown.

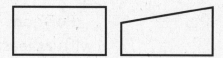

Which attributes do these shapes share?

- Ⓐ opposite sides are of equal length
- Ⓑ number of sides
- Ⓒ all sides are of equal length
- Ⓓ number of angles
- Ⓔ at least one right angle

5 Which quadrilateral always has 4 sides of equal length, but does not always have 4 right angles?

- Ⓐ parallelogram
- Ⓒ rhombus
- Ⓑ square
- Ⓓ rectangle

6 Is a rectangle always a square? Write *yes* or *no*.

Spiral Review

7 Write the total number of each kind of angle.

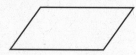

_____ right

_____ less than right

_____ greater than right

8 Write *all* or *some* to complete the sentences.

_____ sides of a rectangle are equal in length.

_____ parallelograms have 2 pairs of sides of equal length.

HMH | **into Math**™

My
Journal

My Progress on Mathematics Standards

The lessons in your *Into Math* book provide instruction for Mathematics Standards for Grade 3. You can use the following pages to reflect on your learning and record your progress through the standards.

As you learn new concepts, reflect on this learning. Consider inserting a check mark if you understand the concepts or inserting a question mark if you have questions or need help.

	Student Edition Lessons	My Progress
Domain: OPERATIONS AND ALGEBRAIC THINKING		
Cluster: Represent and solve problems involving multiplication and division.		
Interpret products of whole numbers, e.g., interpret 5×7 as the total number of objects in 5 groups of 7 objects each.	1.1, 1.2, 5.3	
Interpret whole-number quotients of whole numbers, e.g., interpret $56 \div 8$ as the number of objects in each share when 56 objects are partitioned equally into 8 shares, or as a number of shares when 56 objects are partitioned into equal shares of 8 objects each.	6.2, 6.3, 6.6	

	Student Edition Lessons	My Progress
Use multiplication and division within 100 to solve word problems in situations involving equal groups, arrays, and measurement quantities, e.g., by using drawings and equations with a symbol for the unknown number to represent the problem.	1.3, 1.5, 1.6, 3.1, 3.2, 3.3, 5.4, 6.1, 6.4, 6.5, 7.3, 7.4, 7.5, 8.3, 8.4, 8.5	
Determine the unknown whole number in a multiplication or division equation relating three whole numbers.	7.6, 8.2, 8.3	
Cluster: Understand properties of multiplication and the relationship between multiplication and division.		
Apply properties of operations as strategies to multiply and divide.	1.4, 4.1, 4.2, 4.3, 4.4, 4.5, 4.6, 4.7, 5.1, 5.2, 6.7, 7.6	
Understand division as an unknown-factor problem.	7.1, 8.2	

	Student Edition Lessons	My Progress
Cluster: Multiply and divide within 100.		
Fluently multiply and divide within 100, using strategies such as the relationship between multiplication and division (e.g., knowing that $8 \times 5 = 40$, one knows $40 \div 5 = 8$) or properties of operations. By the end of Grade 3, know from memory all products of two one-digit numbers.	4.4, 4.5, 4.6, 7.2, 7.3, 7.4, 7.5, 7.7	
Cluster: Solve problems involving the four operations, and identify and explain patterns in arithmetic.		
Solve two-step word problems using the four operations. Represent these problems using equations with a letter standing for the unknown quantity. Assess the reasonableness of answers using mental computation and estimation strategies including rounding.	8.4, 8.5, 9.4, 10.6, 18.1	
Identify arithmetic patterns (including patterns in the addition table or multiplication table), and explain them using properties of operations.	4.7, 8.1, 9.1	

	Student Edition Lessons	My Progress
Domain: NUMBER AND OPERATIONS IN BASE TEN		
Cluster: Use place value understanding and properties of operations to perform multi-digit arithmetic.		
Use place value understanding to round whole numbers to the nearest 10 or 100.	9.5, 9.6	
Fluently add and subtract within 1000 using strategies and algorithms based on place value, properties of operations, and/or the relationship between addition and subtraction.	9.2, 9.3, 10.1, 10.2, 10.3, 10.4, 10.5	
Multiply one-digit whole numbers by multiples of 10 in the range 10–90 (e.g., 9×80, 5×60) using strategies based on place value and properties of operations.	5.1, 5.2, 5.3, 5.4	

	Student Edition Lessons	My Progress
Domain: NUMBER AND OPERATIONS–FRACTIONS		
Cluster: Develop understanding of fractions as numbers.		
Understand a fraction $\frac{1}{b}$ as the quantity formed by 1 part when a whole is partitioned into b equal parts; understand a fraction $\frac{a}{b}$ as the quantity formed by a parts of size $\frac{1}{b}$.	13.1, 13.2, 13.3, 13.6	
Understand a fraction as a number on the number line; represent fractions on a number line diagram.		
• Represent a fraction $\frac{1}{b}$ on a number line diagram by defining the interval from 0 to 1 as the whole and partitioning it into b equal parts. Recognize that each part has size $\frac{1}{b}$ and that the endpoint of the part based at 0 locates the number $\frac{1}{b}$ on the number line.	13.4	
• Represent a fraction $\frac{a}{b}$ on a number line diagram by marking off a lengths $\frac{1}{b}$ from 0. Recognize that the resulting interval has size $\frac{a}{b}$ and that its endpoint locates the number $\frac{a}{b}$ on the number line.	13.4, 13.6	

	Student Edition Lessons	My Progress
Explain equivalence of fractions in special cases, and compare fractions by reasoning about their size.	15.1	
• Understand two fractions as equivalent (equal) if they are the same size, or the same point on a number line.	13.5, 16.1, 16.2, 16.3	
• Recognize and generate simple equivalent fractions, e.g., $\frac{1}{2} = \frac{2}{4}$, $\frac{4}{6} = \frac{2}{3}$. Explain why the fractions are equivalent, e.g., by using a visual fraction model.	16.1, 16.2, 16.3	
• Express whole numbers as fractions, and recognize fractions that are equivalent to whole numbers.	13.5	
• Compare two fractions with the same numerator or the same denominator by reasoning about their size. Recognize that comparisons are valid only when the two fractions refer to the same whole. Record the results of comparisons with the symbols $>$, $=$, or $<$, and justify the conclusions, e.g., by using a visual fraction model.	15.1, 15.2, 15.3, 15.4	

Interactive Standards

	Student Edition Lessons	My Progress
Domain: MEASUREMENT AND DATA		
Cluster: Solve problems involving measurement and estimation of intervals of time, liquid volumes, and masses of objects.		
Tell and write time to the nearest minute and measure time intervals in minutes. Solve word problems involving addition and subtraction of time intervals in minutes, e.g., by representing the problem on a number line diagram.	12.1, 12.2, 12.3, 12.4, 12.5	
Measure and estimate liquid volumes and masses of objects using standard units of grams (g), kilograms (kg), and liters (l). Add, subtract, multiply, or divide to solve one-step word problems involving masses or volumes that are given in the same units.	17.1, 17.2, 17.3	
Cluster: Represent and interpret data.		
Draw a scaled picture graph and a scaled bar graph to represent a data set with several categories. Solve one- and two-step "how many more" and "how many less" problems using information presented in scaled bar graphs.	18.1, 18.2, 18.3, 18.4, 18.7	
Generate measurement data by measuring lengths using rulers marked with halves and fourths of an inch. Show the data by making a line plot, where the horizontal scale is marked off in appropriate units—whole numbers, halves, or quarters.	13.7, 18.5, 18.6	

	Student Edition Lessons	My Progress
Cluster: Geometric measurement: understand concepts of area and relate area to multiplication and to addition.		
Recognize area as an attribute of plane figures and understand concepts of area measurement.	2.1	
• A square with side length 1 unit, called "a unit square," is said to have "one square unit" of area, and can be used to measure area.	2.1	
• A plane figure which can be covered without gaps or overlaps by *n* unit squares is said to have an area of *n* square units.	2.2	
Measure areas by counting unit squares (square cm, square m, square in, square ft, and improvised units).	2.2	

	Student Edition Lessons	My Progress
Relate area to the operations of multiplication and addition.	2.3	
• Find the area of a rectangle with whole-number side lengths by tiling it, and show that the area is the same as would be found by multiplying the side lengths.	2.3	
• Multiply side lengths to find areas of rectangles with whole-number side lengths in the context of solving real world and mathematical problems, and represent whole-number products as rectangular areas in mathematical reasoning.	2.4	
• Use tiling to show in a concrete case that the area of a rectangle with whole-number side lengths a and $b + c$ is the sum of $a \times b$ and $a \times c$. Use area models to represent the distributive property in mathematical reasoning.	2.5	
• Recognize area as additive. Find areas of rectilinear figures by decomposing them into non-overlapping rectangles and adding the areas of the non-overlapping parts, applying this technique to solve real world problems.	2.5	

	Student Edition Lessons	My Progress
Cluster: Geometric measurement: recognize perimeter as an attribute of plane figures and distinguish between linear and area measures.		
Solve real world and mathematical problems involving perimeters of polygons, including finding the perimeter given the side lengths, finding an unknown side length, and exhibiting rectangles with the same perimeter and different areas or with the same area and different perimeters.	11.1, 11.2, 11.3, 11.4, 11.5	
Domain: GEOMETRY		
Cluster: Reason with shapes and their attributes.		
Understand that shapes in different categories (e.g., rhombuses, rectangles, and others) may share attributes (e.g., having four sides), and that the shared attributes can define a larger category (e.g., quadrilaterals). Recognize rhombuses, rectangles, and squares as examples of quadrilaterals, and draw examples of quadrilaterals that do not belong to any of these subcategories.	19.1, 19.2, 19.3, 19.4, 20.1, 20.2, 20.3	
Partition shapes into parts with equal areas. Express the area of each part as a unit fraction of the whole.	13.1, 13.2, 14.1, 14.2, 14.3	

My Learning Summary

As you learn about new concepts, complete a learning summary for each module. A learning summary can include drawings, examples, non-examples, and terminology. It's your learning summary, so show or include information that will help you.

At the end of each module, you will have a summary you can reference to review content for a module test and help you make connections with related math concepts.

My Learning Summary

My Learning Summary

My Learning Summary

My Learning Summary

My Learning Summary

My Learning Summary

My Learning Summary

My Learning Summary

My Learning Summary

My Learning Summary

My Learning Summary

My Learning Summary

My Learning Summary

My Learning Summary

My Learning Summary

Name

My Learning Summary

My Learning Summary

My Learning Summary

My Learning Summary

My Learning Summary

As you learn about each new term, add notes, drawings, or sentences in the space next to the definition. Doing so will help you remember what each term means.

Pronunciation Key

a add, map	ē equal, tree	m move, seem	o͞o pool, food	u̇ pull, book
ā ace, rate	f fit, half	n nice, tin	p pit, stop	û(r) burn, term
â(r) care, air	g go, log	ng ring, song	r run, poor	yo͞o fuse, few
ä palm, father	h hope, hate	o odd, hot	s see, pass	v vain, eve
b bat, rub	i it, give	ō open, so	sh sure, rush	w win, away
ch check, catch	ī ice, write	ô order, jaw	t talk, sit	y yet, yearn
d dog, rod	j joy, ledge	oi oil, boy	th thin, both	z zest, muse
e end, pet	k cool, take	ou pout, now	th this, bathe	zh vision,
	l look, rule	o͝o took, full	u up, done	pleasure

ə the schwa, an unstressed vowel representing the sound spelled *a* in *above*, *e* in *sicken*, *i* in *possible*, *o* in *melon*, *u* in *circus*

Other symbols:
- • separates words into syllables
- ′ indicates stress on a syllable

A

My Vocabulary Summary

addend [aˊdend] Any of the numbers that are added in addition

sumando Cualquiera de los números que se suman en una operación de suma

addition [ə•dishˊən] The process of finding the total number of items when two or more groups of items are joined; the opposite operation of subtraction

suma Proceso de hallar la cantidad total de objetos cuando se unen dos o más grupos de objetos; operación inversa de la resta

Interactive Glossary

My Vocabulary Summary

a.m. [ā•em] The time after midnight and before noon

a. m. Se usa para indicar una hora entre la medianoche y el mediodía

angle [ɑng´gəl] A shape formed by two rays that share an endpoint

ángulo Figura formada por dos semirrectas que tienen un extremo común

area [âr´ē•ə] The measure of the number of unit squares needed to cover a surface

área Medida de la cantidad de cuadrados de una unidad que se necesitan para cubrir una superficie

array [ə•rā´] A set of objects arranged in rows and columns

matriz Conjunto de objetos agrupados en hileras y columnas

Associative Property of Addition
[ə•sō´shē•āt•iv präp´ər•tē əv ə•dish´ən]
The property that states that you can group addends in different ways and still get the same sum

propiedad asociativa de la suma
Propiedad que dice que cambiar el modo en que se agrupan los sumandos no cambia la suma

Associative Property of Multiplication
[ə•sō´shē•āt•iv präp´ər•tē əv mul•tə•pli•kā´shən] The property that states that when the grouping of factors is changed, the product remains the same

propiedad asociativa de la multiplicación Propiedad que dice que cambiar el modo en que se agrupan los factores no cambia el producto

B

bar graph [bär graf] A graph that uses bars to show data

gráfica de barras Gráfica que muestra datos por medio de barras

Interactive Glossary

C

capacity [kə•pas´i•tē] The amount a container can hold when filled

capacidad Cantidad que puede contener un recipiente cuando se llena

centimeter (cm) [sen´tə•mēt•ər] A metric unit that is used to measure length or distance

centímetro (cm) Unidad del sistema métrico que se usa para medir la longitud o la distancia

closed shape [klōzd shāp] A shape that begins and ends at the same point

figura cerrada Figura que comienza en un punto y termina en el mismo punto

Commutative Property of Addition
[kə•myo͞ot´ə•tiv präp´ər•tē əv ə•dish´ən]
The property that states that you can add two or more numbers in any order and get the same sum

propiedad conmutativa de la suma Propiedad que dice que dos números se pueden sumar en cualquier orden y la suma que se obtiene es la misma

© Houghton Mifflin Harcourt Publishing Company

Commutative Property of Multiplication

[kə•myo͞ ot´ə•tiv präp´ər•tē əv mul•tə•pli•kā´shən] The property that states that you can multiply two factors in any order and get the same product

propiedad conmutativa de la multiplicación Propiedad que dice que dos factores se pueden multiplicar en cualquier orden y el producto que se obtiene es el mismo

compare [kəm•pâr´] To describe whether numbers are equal to, less than, or greater than each other

comparar Describir si los números son iguales entre sí o si uno es menor o mayor que el otro

compatible numbers [kəm•pat´ə•bəl num´bərz] Numbers that are easy to compute with mentally

números compatibles Números con los que es fácil hacer cálculos mentales

counting number [kount´ing num´bər] A whole number that can be used to count a set of objects (1, 2, 3, 4, …)

número natural Número entero que se puede usar para contar un conjunto de objetos (1, 2, 3, 4, …)

Interactive Glossary

D

data [dāt´ə] Information collected about people or things

datos Información recopilada sobre personas o cosas

denominator [dē•näm´ə•nāt•ər] The part of a fraction below the line, which tells how many equal parts there are in the whole or in the group

denominador Parte de una fracción que está debajo de la línea de fracción y que indica cuántas partes iguales hay en el entero o en el grupo

difference [dif´ər•əns] The answer to a subtraction problem

diferencia Resultado de una resta

digits [dij´its] The symbols 0, 1, 2, 3, 4, 5, 6, 7, 8, and 9

dígitos Los símbolos 0, 1, 2, 3, 4, 5, 6, 7, 8 y 9

Distributive Property [di•strib′yoo•tiv präp′ər•tē] The property that states that multiplying a sum by a number is the same as multiplying each addend by the number and then adding the products

propiedad distributiva Propiedad que dice que multiplicar una suma por un número es lo mismo que multiplicar cada sumando por ese número y después sumar los productos

divide [də•vīd′] To separate into equal groups; the opposite operation of multiplication

dividir Separar en grupos iguales; operación inversa de la multiplicación

dividend [div′ə•dend] The number that is to be divided in a division problem

dividendo Número que se divide en una división

division [də•vizh′ən] The process of sharing a number of items to find how many equal groups can be made or how many items will be in each equal group; the opposite operation of multiplication

división Proceso de repartir un número de artículos para calcular cuántos grupos iguales se pueden formar o cuántos artículos habrá en cada uno de esos grupos iguales; operación inversa de la multiplicación

Interactive Glossary

divisor [de•vī′zər] The number that divides the dividend

divisor Número entre el cual se divide el dividendo

doubles [dub′əlz] Pairs of addends that are the same

dobles Pares de sumandos iguales

E

eighths [āt̄ths] Eight equal parts of a whole or a group

octavos Ocho partes iguales de un entero o de un grupo

elapsed time [ē•lapst′ tīm] The time that passes from the start of an activity to the end of that activity

tiempo transcurrido Tiempo que transcurre desde el comienzo de una actividad hasta su finalización

endpoint [end′point] The point at either end of a line segment

extremo Puntos que se encuentran en los límites de un segmento

equal groups [ēʹkwəl gro͞opz] Groups that have the same number of objects

grupos iguales Grupos que tienen la misma cantidad de objetos

equal parts [ēʹkwəl pärts] Parts that are exactly the same size

partes iguales Partes que tienen exactamente el mismo tamaño

equal to (=) [ēʹkwəl to͞o] Having the same value

igual a (=) Que tiene el mismo valor

equation [ē•kwāʹzhən] A number sentence that uses the equal sign to show that two amounts are equal

ecuación Enunciado numérico en el que se usa el signo de la igualdad para mostrar que dos cantidades son iguales

equivalent [ē•kwivʹə•lənt] Two or more sets that name the same amount

equivalente Dos o más conjuntos que indican la misma cantidad

Interactive Glossary

equivalent fractions [ē•kwiv´ə•lənt frak´shənz] Two or more fractions that name the same amount

fracciones equivalentes Dos o más fracciones que indican la misma cantidad

estimate (noun) [es´tə•mit] A number close to an exact amount

estimación Número cercano a una cantidad exacta

estimate (verb) [es´tə•māt] To find about how many or how much

estimar Hallar la cantidad aproximada de algo

even [ē´vən] A whole number that has a 0, 2, 4, 6, or 8 in the ones place

par Número entero que tiene un 0, 2, 4, 6 u 8 en el lugar de las unidades

expanded form [ek•span´did fôrm] A way to write numbers by showing the value of each digit

forma desarrollada Manera de escribir los números de forma que muestren el valor de cada uno de los dígitos

My Vocabulary Summary

F

factor [fak´tər] A number that is multiplied by another number to find a product

factor Número que se multiplica por otro para obtener un producto

---

foot (ft) [fŏŏt] A customary unit used to measure length or distance;
1 foot = 12 inches

pie Unidad del sistema usual que se usa para medir la longitud o la distancia;
1 pie = 12 pulgadas

---

fourths [fôrths] Four equal parts of a whole or a group

cuartos Cuatro partes iguales de un entero o de un grupo

---

fraction [frak´shən] A number that names part of a whole or part of a group

fracción Número que indica una parte de un entero o una parte de un grupo

---

fraction greater than 1 [frak´shən grāt´ər than wun] A number which has a numerator that is greater than its denominator

fracción mayor que 1 Fracción cuyo numerador es mayor que su denominador

Interactive Glossary

frequency table [frē′kwən•sē tā′bəl] A table that uses numbers to record data

tabla de frecuencia Tabla en la que se usan números para registrar datos

G

gram (g) [gram] A metric unit that is used to measure mass

gramo (g) Unidad del sistema métrico que se usa para medir la masa

greater than (>) [grāt′ər than] A symbol used to compare two numbers when the greater number is given first

mayor que (>) Símbolo que se usa para comparar dos números cuando el número mayor se da primero

growing pattern [grō′ing pat′ərn] A pattern in which the number changes by the same amount from one number to the next

patrón en aumento Patrón en el cual el número cambia por la misma cantidad de un número al siguiente

H

half hour [haf our] 30 minutes

media hora 30 minutos

halves [havz] Two equal parts of a whole or a group

mitades Dos partes iguales de un entero o de un grupo

hexagon [hek´sə•gän] A polygon with six sides and six angles

hexágono Polígono que tiene seis lados y seis ángulos

horizontal bar graph [hôr•i•zänt´l bär graf] A bar graph in which the bars go from left to right

gráfica de barras horizontales Gráfica de barras en la que las barras van de izquierda a derecha

I

Identity Property of Addition
[ī•den´tə•tē präp´ər•tē əv ə•dish´ən]
The property that states that when you add zero to a number, the result is that number

propiedad de identidad de la suma
Propiedad que dice que cuando se suma cero a un número, el resultado es ese número

Identity Property of Multiplication
[ī•den´tə•tē präp´ər•tē əv mul•tə•pli•kā´shən]
The property that states that the product of any number and 1 is that number

propiedad de identidad de la multiplicación Propiedad que dice que el producto de cualquier número por 1 es ese número

inch (in.) [inch] A customary unit used to measure length or distance

pulgada (pulg) Unidad del sistema usual que se usa para medir la longitud o la distancia

inverse operations [in´vûrs äp•ə•rā´shənz]
Opposite operations, or operations that undo one another, such as addition and subtraction or multiplication and division

operaciones inversas Operaciones opuestas u operaciones que se cancelan entre sí, como la suma y la resta o la multiplicación y la división

K

key [kē] The part of a map or graph that explains the symbols

clave Parte de un mapa o una gráfica que explica los símbolos

kilogram (kg) [kil´ō•gram] A metric unit used to measure mass; 1 kilogram = 1,000 grams

kilogramo (kg) Unidad del sistema métrico que se usa para medir la masa; 1 kilogramo = 1,000 gramos

L

length [lengkth] The measurement of the distance between two points

longitud Medida de la distancia entre dos puntos

Interactive Glossary

less than (<) [les <u>th</u>an] A symbol used to compare two numbers when the lesser number is given first

menor que (<) Símbolo que se usa para comparar dos números cuando el número menor se da primero

---

line plot [līn plot] A graph that records each piece of data on a number line

diagrama de puntos Gráfica que registra cada uno de los datos en una recta numérica

---

line segment [līn seg´mənt] A part of a line that includes two points, called endpoints, and all the points between them

segmento Parte de una línea que incluye dos puntos, llamados extremos, y todos los puntos entre ellos

My Vocabulary Summary

liquid volume [lik´wid väl´yo͞om] The amount of liquid in a container

volumen de un líquido Cantidad de líquido que hay en un recipiente

liter (L) [lēt´ər] A metric unit used to measure capacity and liquid volume; 1 liter = 1,000 milliliters

litro (L) Unidad del sistema métrico que se usa para medir la capacidad y el volumen de un líquido; 1 litro = 1,000 mililitros

M

mass [mɑs] The amount of matter in an object

masa Cantidad de materia que hay en un objeto

meter (m) [mēt´ər] A metric unit used to measure length or distance; 1 meter = 100 centimeters

metro (m) Unidad del sistema métrico que se usa para medir la longitud o la distancia; 1 metro = 100 centímetros

Interactive Glossary

midnight [mid′nīt] 12:00 at night

medianoche 12:00 de la noche

---

milliliter (mL) [mil′i•lēt•ər] A metric unit used to measure capacity and liquid volume

mililitro (mL) Unidad del sistema métrico que se usa para medir la capacidad y el volumen de un líquido

---

minute (min) [min′it] A unit used to measure short amounts of time; in one minute, the minute hand on an analog clock moves from one mark to the next

minuto (min) Unidad que se usa para medir cantidades cortas de tiempo; en un minuto, el minutero de un reloj analógico se mueve de una marca a la siguiente

---

mixed number [mikst num′bər] A number represented by a whole number and a fraction

número mixto Una cantidad que se da como un número entero y una fracción

---

multiple [mul′tə•pəl] A number that is the product of two counting numbers

múltiplo Número que es el producto de dos números naturales

multiplication [mul•tə•pli•kā´shən] A process to find the total number of items in equal-sized groups, or to find the total number of items in a given number of groups when each group contains the same number of items; the opposite operation of division

multiplicación El proceso por el cual se halla el número total de elementos en grupos del mismo tamaño o el número total de elementos en un número dado de grupos cuando todos los grupos tienen el mismo número de elementos; operación inversa de la división

multiply [mul´tə•plī] To combine equal groups to find how many in all; the opposite operation of division

multiplicar Combinar grupos iguales para hallar cuántos hay en total; la operación opuesta a la división

N

noon [no͞on] 12:00 in the day

mediodía Las 12:00 del día

number line [num´bər līn] A line on which numbers can be located

recta numérica Una línea en la que se pueden ubicar los números

Interactive Glossary

numerator [nōō´mər•āt•ər] The part of a fraction above the line, which tells how many parts are being counted

numerador El número que está arriba de la barra en una fracción y que indica cuántas partes del entero o del grupo se consideran

O

odd [od] A whole number that has a 1, 3, 5, 7, or 9 in the ones place

impar Número entero que tiene un 1, 3, 5, 7, u 9 en el lugar de las unidades

open shape [ō´pən shāp] A shape that does not begin and end at the same point

figura abierta Figura que comienza en un punto pero no termina en ese mismo punto

P

parallel lines [pâr´ə•lel līnz] Lines in the same plane that never cross and are always the same distance apart

líneas paralelas Líneas que están en el mismo plano, que no se cortan nunca y que siempre están separadas por la misma distancia

parallelogram [pâr•ə•lel´ə•gram]
A quadrilateral whose opposite sides
are parallel and of equal length

paralelogramo Un cuadrilátero con lados
opuestos paralelos y de igual longitud

---

pattern [pat´ərn] An ordered set of
numbers or objects in which the order
helps you predict what will come next

patrón Conjunto ordenado de números
u objetos en el que el orden ayuda a
predecir el siguiente número u objeto

---

pentagon [pen´tə•gän] A polygon with
five sides and five angles

pentágono Polígono que tiene cinco
lados y cinco ángulos

---

perimeter [pə•rim´ə•tər] The distance
around a figure

perímetro Distancia del contorno de
una figura

Interactive Glossary

picture graph [pik´chər graf] A graph that uses pictures to show and compare information

pictografía Gráfica en la que se usan dibujos para mostrar y comparar información

place value [plās val´yo͞o] The value of each digit in a number, based on the location of the digit

valor posicional Valor de cada uno de los dígitos de un número, según el lugar que ocupa en el número

plane shape [plān shāp] A shape on a flat surface that is formed by curves, line segments, or both

figura plana Figura en un plano que está formada por curvas, segmentos o ambos

p.m. [pē•em] The time after noon and before midnight

p. m. Se usa para indicar una hora después del mediodía y antes de la medianoche

My Vocabulary Summary

polygon [päl´i•gän] A closed plane shape with straight sides that are line segments

polígono Figura plana y cerrada que tiene lados rectos que son segmentos

product [präd´əkt] The answer in a multiplication problem

producto Resultado de una multiplicación

Q

quadrilateral [kwäd•ri•lat´ər•əl] A polygon with four sides and four angles

cuadrilátero Polígono que tiene cuatro lados y cuatro ángulos

quarter hour [kwôrt´ər our] 15 minutes

cuarto de hora 15 minutos

quotient [kwō´shənt] The number that results from dividing

cociente Número que resulta de una división

Interactive Glossary

R

rectangle [rek´tang•gəl] A quadrilateral with two pairs of parallel sides, two pairs of sides of equal length, and four right angles

rectángulo Cuadrilátero que tiene dos pares de lados paralelos, dos pares de lados de la misma longitud y cuatro ángulos rectos

regroup [rē•groop´] To exchange amounts of equal value to rename a number

reagrupar Intercambiar cantidades de valores equivalentes para volver a escribir un número

related facts [ri•lāt´id fakts] A set of related addition and subtraction, or multiplication and division, equations

operaciones relacionadas Conjunto de enunciados numéricos relacionados de suma y resta o multiplicación y división

rhombus [räm´bəs] A quadrilateral with two pairs of parallel sides and four sides of equal length

rombo Cuadrilátero que tiene dos pares de lados paralelos y cuatro lados de la misma longitud

right angle [rīt ang´gəl] An angle that forms a square corner

ángulo recto Ángulo que forma una esquina cuadrada

round [round] To replace a number with another number that tells about how many or how much

redondear Reemplazar un número por otro que indique una cantidad aproximada

rule [rool] An instruction that tells you the correct way to do something

regla Instrucción que indica la manera correcta de hacer algo

S

scale [skāl] The numbers placed at fixed distances on a graph to help label the graph

escala Números que están ubicados a una distancia fija entre sí en una gráfica que ayudan a rotular esa gráfica

Interactive Glossary

side [sīd] A straight line segment in a polygon

lado Segmento recto de un polígono

sixths [siksths] Six equal parts of a whole or a group

sextos Seis partes iguales de un entero o de un grupo

square [skwâr] A quadrilateral with two pairs of parallel sides, four sides of equal length, and four right angles

cuadrado Cuadrilátero que tiene dos pares de lados paralelos, cuatro lados de la misma longitud y cuatro ángulos rectos

square unit [skwâr yōō′nit] A unit used to measure area such as square foot, square meter, and so on

unidad cuadrada Unidad del sistema usual que se usa para medir el área

standard form [stan′dərd fôrm] A way to write numbers by using the digits 0–9, with each digit having a place value

forma normal Manera de escribir los números con los dígitos del 0 al 9 de forma que cada dígito ocupe un valor posicional

My Vocabulary Summary

subtraction [səb•trak′shən] The process of finding how many are left when a number of items are taken away from a group of items; the process of finding the difference when two groups are compared; the opposite operation of addition

resta Proceso de hallar cuántos objetos sobran cuando se quita un número de objetos de un grupo; proceso de hallar la diferencia cuando se comparan dos grupos; operación inversa de la suma

sum [sum] The answer to an addition problem

suma o total Resultado de una suma

T

tally table [tal′ē tā′bəl] A table that uses tally marks to record data

tabla de conteo Tabla en la que se usan marcas de conteo para registrar datos

thirds [thûrdz] Three equal parts of a whole or a group

tercios Tres partes iguales de un entero o de un grupo

Interactive Glossary

trapezoid [trap´i•zoid] *exclusive* A quadrilateral with exactly one pair of parallel sides

trapecio *exclusivo* Cuadrilátero que tiene exactamente un par de lados paralelos

trapezoid [trap´i•zoid] *inclusive* A quadrilateral with at least one pair of parallel sides

trapecio *inclusivo* Cuadrilátero con un par de lados paralelos

triangle [trī´ang•gəl] A polygon with three sides and three angles

triángulo Polígono que tiene tres lados y tres ángulos

two-dimensional shape [t$\overline{oo}$ də•men´shə•nəl shāp] A shape that has only length and width

figura bidimensional Figura que solamente tiene longitud y ancho

U

unit fraction [y$\overline{oo}$´nit frak´shən] A fraction that has 1 as its top number, or numerator

fracción unitaria Fracción que tiene un número 1 como numerador

My Vocabulary Summary

unit square [yōō′nit skwâr] A square with a side length of 1 unit, used to measure area

cuadrado de una unidad Cuadrado cuya longitud de lado mide 1 unidad y se usa para medir el área

V

Venn diagram [ven dī′ə•gram] A diagram that shows relationships among sets of things

diagrama de Venn Diagrama que muestra las relaciones entre conjuntos de cosas

vertex [vûr′teks] The point at which two rays of an angle or two (or more) line segments meet in a plane shape

vértice Punto en el que se encuentran dos semirrectas de un ángulo o dos (o más) segmentos en una figura plana

vertical bar graph [vûr′ti•kəl bär graf] A bar graph in which the bars go up from the bottom to the top

gráfica de barras verticales Gráfica de barras en la que las barras van de abajo hacia arriba

Interactive Glossary

W

whole [hōl] All of the parts of a shape or group

entero Todas las partes de una figura o grupo

whole number [hōl num'bər] One of the numbers 0, 1, 2, 3, 4, …; the set of whole numbers goes on without end

número entero Uno de los números 0, 1, 2, 3, 4, …; el conjunto de números enteros es infinito

word form [wûrd fôrm] A way to write numbers by using words

en palabras Manera de escribir los números usando palabras

Z

Zero Property of Multiplication [zē'rō präp'ər•tē əv mul•tə•pli•kā'shən] The property that states that the product of zero and any number is zero

propiedad del cero de la multiplicación Propiedad que dice que el producto de cero y cualquier número es cero

Table of Measures

LENGTH

Metric	Customary
1 centimeter (cm) = 10 millimeters (mm)	1 foot (ft) = 12 inches (in.)
1 decimeter (dm) = 10 centimeters (cm)	1 yard (yd) = 3 feet
1 meter (m) = 100 centimeters	1 yard = 36 inches
1 meter (m) = 10 decimeters	1 mile (mi) = 1,760 yards
1 kilometer (km) = 1,000 meters	1 mile = 5,280 feet

CAPACITY AND LIQUID VOLUME

Metric	Customary
1 liter (L) = 1,000 milliliters (mL)	1 pint (pt) = 2 cups (c)
	1 quart (qt) = 2 pints
	1 gallon (gal) = 4 quarts

MASS/WEIGHT

Metric	Customary
1 kilogram (kg) = 1,000 grams	1 pound (lb) = 16 ounces (oz)

TIME

1 minute (min) = 60 seconds (sec)	1 year (yr) = about 52 weeks
1 hour (hr) = 60 minutes	1 year = 12 months (mo)
1 day (d) = 24 hours	1 year = 365 days
1 week (wk) = 7 days	1 leap year = 366 days
	1 decade = 10 years
	1 century = 100 years

MONEY

1 penny = 1 cent (¢)
1 nickel = 5 cents
1 dime = 10 cents
1 quarter = 25 cents
1 half dollar = 50 cents
1 dollar ($) = 100 cents

SYMBOLS

$<$ is less than
$>$ is greater than
$=$ is equal to